# WEEP:

## Why President Donald J. Trump Does Not Deserve A Second Term

Published by:
Old Wharf Publishers
8413 Clematis Lane,
Orlando, Florida 32819.
(407) 580-8664



**WEEP: Why President Donald Trump Does Not Deserve A Second Term.**

Dedicated to:

My grandchildren, Malcolm, Eloise and Emmeline, for a better life

# Acknowledgment

I am grateful to my wife, Heather, for painstakingly reading the manuscript and correcting the proofs. Her patience, diligence and forbearance showed on every page as we tried to get the book out to you in the brevity of time we had to work with. This is a very special time for us as the book's publication coincided with the celebration of our 38 years of marriage. Her profound dedication to this work made my task less burdensome.

# CONTENT

*The word of the LORD came to me:* ² *"Son of man, speak to your people and say to them: 'When I bring the sword against a land, and the people of the land choose one of their men and make him their watchman,* ³ *and he sees the sword coming against the land and blows the trumpet to warn the people,* ⁴ *then if anyone hears the trumpet but does not heed the warning and the sword comes and takes their life, their blood will be on their own head.* ⁵ *Since they heard the sound of the trumpet but did not heed the warning, their blood will be on their own head. If they had heeded the warning, they would have saved themselves.* ⁶ *But if the watchman sees the sword coming and does not blow the trumpet to warn the people and the sword comes and takes someone's life, that person's life will be taken because of their sin, but I will hold the watchman accountable for their blood.'*

**(Ezekiel 33: 1-6-New International Version)**

# INTRODUCTION

On December 2006, I visited the Turkey Lake Post Office in Orlando. I had been to a United States post office before, but this day was different. It held a particular significance which dawned on me as I drove to my destination. I was mailing a document that would alter my life and that of my family forever, hopefully for good. I was going to mail our application to become citizens of the United States.

When I mailed the document a great feeling of relief wafted over me. Contrary to what many may think, it was not an easy decision to make. My two children were young and filled with the enthusiasm of living in a new country with all the opportunities that this could present. My wife was seized of the significance of the decision that we had taken knowing that we could have a bright future in America.

I too was seized of the significance of the moment but was a bit diffident in coming to the decision. I think I speak for a lot of immigrants when I say that that taking an oath to become a citizen of another country is not as easy as it may appear. It begets some guilt that you are abandoning the country of your birth. That you are being unpatriotic.

After much wrestling, I finally came to the conclusion that this is what I had to do. While I did not take any comfort from it, I had heard of a statement attributed to the English conversationalist Samuel Johnson, that patriotism is often the refuge of scoundrels. I know I had to make a decision in tandem with what was in the best interests of my family.

Looking back, I am glad I did. My children have done excellently and are making their contribution to society.

We had been in the country five years before filing our application so we had a good idea of what the future could portend. As time transpired, I have discovered that my love and concern for Jamaica has not dimmed. It never dimmed. In fact, it has burned brighter than perhaps it was before.

Why America? I had visited the United States many times before. When I journeyed to the post office, I believed, and still do, that America is a remarkable place. It is one of the grandest experiments in nation building that the world has ever seen. My family and I chose America for the reason that so many people from all over the world have-to seek a better future in a land which promised much. There are many who believe that if they cannot make it in America, they cannot make it anywhere else. As the quintessential immigrant nation, America has really been to many what Ronald Reagan called the shining city on a hill, or a place where Emma Lazarus's tired, poor and huddled masses can breathe and find freedom.

It is truly a remarkable nation whose malleability has allowed it to become the only remaining superpower in the world. But, as I write in this 244th year of the country's independence, and in the midst of one of the worst pandemics it has ever faced, the report card on the state of the American union is not good. In fact, today America is a broken, divided and humiliated nation. The country is more polarized than it has ever been, perhaps even more than during the Civil War in which more Americans were killed than in all the wars it has fought.

Today, the reasons for our polarization and brokenness as a society may not be as clear cut as they were under the Civil War. There are diverse reasons for the divisions that plague the nation. From income inequality, to systemic racism, to the rise of ethnic, supremacist and xenophobic dispositions, to rotting infrastructure especially in deprived inner-city communities, to its loss of respectability around the world, America is a big social powder keg waiting to explode.

There are any number of reasons why we got here. I will explore some of them here and weep as I do so. I say weep, because no one who has understood the promise of the experiment called America, who truly understand what America means to the world, can help but have sorrow for the sad spectacle that America has become to the world. At any given time, the world yearns for compassionate leadership from America, but what we are witnessing is the slow death of American compassion, domestically and internationally.

And it is not only that the country is under the existential threat of a pandemic. What we are witnessing is a nation in decline, in retreat from its responsibilities as a global power. We are witnessing a nation that has been forced to become aware of the treachery of its history in its treatment of minority groups-blacks, Latinos and its indigenous populations. It is in the grip of a federal leadership headed by a president whose demagoguery knows no bounds, and whose utterances and actions have been a source of embarrassment to it. It is not hyperbole to say that under the present Trump Administration, a proud and great nation has been reduced to the status of a frightened and whimpering child.

Why this book? What follows here is no social, political, economical or even psychological treatise on what ails America. Much has been written about this. Search engines abound with analyses of any of these subjects which the interested person can consult. But I have been bewildered at how many Americans are oblivious of the perils that face the nation; of the existential threats that imperil its democratic way of life; of the nonchalance with which many regard the erosion of the bedrock of compassion which has been essential to American soft power in the world. We are witnessing the death of American compassion and the imbecility of leadership that promotes an America which the Founding Fathers would not recognize.

*Weep* is my personal assessment of America seen through the eyes of an immigrant. It is in fact an immigrant's lament. But it is also a warning of what can happen to the American experiment if we do not wake up and see the grave dangers that the nation faces as it gets another chance to move in a new direction on November 3, 2020. The next presidential elections will be the most decisive in recent memory. Is the American electorate sufficiently aware of what is at stake to change course or is it prepared to maintain the status quo and have four more years or worse of what the country has been experiencing?

I offer what I have gleaned with all humility. Humility is an essential characteristic of sorrow. It is not sorrow that I chose to live here or even over how things have turned out. Educationally and economically, my family and I have done well. But it is sorrow over what we have become and even more so fast becoming; over the blindness of national leadership that will cause more unnecessary pain on the country (the coronavirus is still raging); sorrow over the debasement of its national institutions and the threat to its democratic way of life; sorrow over the continuing marginalization of the poor and weak in American society and the shameful enrichment of the wealthiest; and sorrow that a once proud nation is being made the laughing stock of the world by the depredations, impetuosity and intemperance of a president who seems to believe more in theatrics than in the principles of real governance.

So, while I weep there is hope, for that is the other characteristic of genuine sorrow. It is hope that we can course correct and strive for a better future. In this book I have set out many reasons why I do not believe that president Trump deserves a second term. I have also analyzed what will likely happen to the country if he should get a second term in office. I would not be presumptuous to ask the reader to agree with me on every point but, I crave a fair reading of what I have to say here.

It is only time that can prove much of the prophetic insights that I seek to offer here. There is one overriding motivation on my part and it is that we can create an America that can truly become that beacon on a hill which can be a bright shining light to a perplexed and troubled world. For the world needs America just as America needs the world. Weep with me if you will, but let us at least hold hands in building a better future for this country, the land of the free and home of the brave.

# CHAPTER ONE

## SEND ME YOUR HUDDLED MASSES
### The Immigration Dilemma

*Give me your tired, poor, the huddled masses yearning to breathe free*-Emma Lazarus

I start my reflections with the vexing issue of immigration. I am well aware of how important the immigration question is to the national agenda. In every major discussion, it forces itself to the top three of issues people want to address. This is understandable for if there is anything that defines America it is that it is that of its status as an immigrant nation.

Yet, immigration is problematic and has become increasingly so under President Trump. The last attempt at any semblance of comprehensive immigration reform occurred under President Bush in 2006. The president meant well, but his efforts went up in flames as members of his party abandoned the effort. They feared it was yet another attempt to grant amnesty, which some saw as a repeat of what President Reagan had done in November 1986 when he granted amnesty to three million undocumented immigrants.

Fast forward to now and we find a policy that is in total disarray. The subject has become enmeshed in the country's culture wars and the polarizing and divisive political environment that now prevails in the country. Thus, the sense of humanity that defined it over the years and which was so beautifully and eloquently captured by Emma Lazarus in her poem *The New Colossus*, is being lost.

This is unfortunate and at the same time tragic. Poll after poll reveals that Americans want to have this matter resolved in a comprehensive manner. They are impatient with the patchwork approach and at what they see as the impotence of their political representatives in getting this done. They are particularly perturbed by the polarizing politics which is at the center of their representatives' inability to act. Instinctively, many know that the xenophobic rhetoric is not helpful nor is the crass lack of compassion by which those who want to enter the country are treated.

There are a number of truisms about immigration that can be noted at the outset. A powerful one is that since immigration began in earnest in the 1800's, America has benefitted tremendously from the talent, genius and expertise of those who have left distant lands to come to its shores. People came because America provided a route to prosperity and freedom which in many respects was a distant dream in the countries from which they migrated.

They had one interest which superseded all others: to make a better life for themselves and their families. America held out great hope for them, the hope that they could eke out a living in a land of freedom and opportunity. They believed that if they worked hard and were disciplined and focused enough, they could make it. For many around the world this dream is still alive.

Once immigrants arrive in America, they know that they have not only landed in a land of opportunity, but they have arrived at a place where their best talents could be realized. They only needed an environment that could nurture their talents and help them thrive. This would be an environment in which justice and fairness were essential hallmarks, where people played by the same rules and where there were no impediments in the path of individual progress. In other words, an environment where they could release their God-given potentials without fear and make a real living for themselves and their families.

If there is one thing that defines the new immigrant it is that of an ethic of hard work. Contrary to what many Americans who were born in America think, immigrants are not scroungers or moochers, seeking to feed on the federal generosity of America. In the early days, many arrived from Europe and other countries with just a suitcase or bag with a bundle of clothes and a few dollars in their pockets. Some arrived, and perhaps still arrive, penniless. They knew that from day one if they were to make it, they would have to work hard. Many did not want to suffer the indignity of relying on the largesse of the federal government. If they and their families were going to make it, they would have to bend their shoulders to the wheel.

This they did and, in many instances, it paid rich dividends. As they became citizens, they gained significant foothold in the country they had come to call home. They have involved themselves into every facet of the nation's life-in science, government, defense, to name a few. What I find thoroughly disgusting is to hear remarks by two or three generations of Americans -clearly descended from immigrants- harshly criticizing newly arrived immigrants and urging political leaders and others to erect barriers in their lives.

Obviously, they do not understand their history or did not listen too keenly to the stories that their great grandparents, grandparents and even parents told of their own struggles to make it in America. These struggles are an integral part of familial history which should be emblazoned on the minds of future generations. As the writer of the book of Deuteronomy enjoins about God's word: *"they shall teach them diligently to your children, and shall talk of them when you sit in your house, when you walk by the way, when you lie down, and when you rise up"* (Deuteronomy 6: 7).

I am not sure that those who criticize immigrants today ever read these words from Abraham Lincoln on immigration. No one better understood the pulse of America as an immigrant nation than Abraham Lincoln. In trying to define who the immigrant is today, it is useful to refer to a speech he gave in Chicago, Illinois, on July 10, 1858. When Lincoln gave the speech, America was 30 years old with just about 30 million people. Today the population is over ten times greater, but even then, immigration was a vexing issue. If the challenge was great then, consider where the country is today.

Lincoln began by acknowledging that America is a mighty nation. He paid homage to the Founding Fathers whom he referred to as the "iron men." He acknowledged his generation's gratitude to them for their sacrifice and foresight and sought to connect the new immigrants from Europe with the Founding Fathers. The passage of time and the birth of new generations might have thinned the blood line, but the connection, he conceded, cannot be made through genetics; but through the Declaration of Independence, an overarching moral principle that linked the hearts of liberty loving people everywhere. He said:

> But when they look through that old Declaration of Independence they find that those old men say that 'We hold these truths to be self-evident, that all men are created equal,' and then they feel that that moral sentiment taught in that day evidences their relation to these men, that it is the father of all moral principle in them, and that they have a right to claim it as though they were blood of the blood, and flesh of the men who wrote that Declaration, (loud and long applause) *and so they are.* That is the electric cord in that declaration that links the hearts of patriotic and liberty-loving men together that will link those patriotic hearts as long as the love of freedom exists.in the minds of men throughout the world (applause).

While the love of freedom had universal appeal, America's desire to absorb those who wanted to be free gave it a special standing among the nations of the world. Lincoln was clear that the overriding principle that knit the immigrant with the American native was the equality of men and their desire to be free. There was no equivocation where this was concerned. For him it was more than a philosophical statement. It was a pragmatic one founded on the basic love for freedom and all that it entailed.

Thus, he could insist that those born in America had no more sacred claim on the desire to be free than those who chose to come here. What drew the long and sustained applause was the audience's concurrence with Lincoln that the same patriotic loyalties that inflamed the Founding Fathers was no less than that which burns in the hearts of those who risk all to come to these blessed shores. They must be afforded the same generosity when they arrive as were afforded these "iron men" and their descendants. Lincoln's appeal for a generous regard for the immigrant was deeply rooted in the moral sentiments contained in the founding documents which embraced freedom. It was not freedom as an abstract statement, but that which related to the existential struggle of people everywhere for self-determination and personal progress.

It is still this general sentiment that ought to define America's approach to the immigration problem today. But sadly, it is being lost especially in the Trump era. From national polls on the matter, it is clear that an overwhelming number of Americans agree with Lincoln's view on immigration. It has now become palpably clear that most Americans want to have the problem fixed in a just and comprehensive manner. They do not want unfettered immigration where great swathes of people can live in the country without documentation. But they do not want an approach that merely tinkers with the problem and which does not address it wholesomely. Many know, almost instinctively, that if the problem is not fixed the country's security over the long term will be jeopardized.

From my perspective, and if the polls are to be believed, most Americans are not in sync with the approach of the Trump administration to immigration. The president has taken a very hardened stance which certainly does not comport with the sentiments expressed by Lincoln, the president he falsely likes to favorably compare himself with. His immigration policy is at variance with what many Americans believe to be the value of America as the premier immigrant nation.

Indeed, his treatment of many Latin Americans on the Southern border makes the point well. Prior to Trump, as far as I know, there was nothing in the immigration lexicon of America that supported any notion that America should be walled from the rest of the world. Yet, President Trump's obsession in building a wall between America and Mexico has left many astonished at the radical, and sometimes vile way, in which he has pursued this intention.

Most offensive has been his cruel treatment of Latin American immigrants in his perverse policy of separating children from their families once they crossed into the USA. If there is anything that should indicate that Trump does not deserve a second term, this is it. Research has indicated that this policy was more premeditated and systematic than one might have thought. Yet, there was no deep thought given to the fact of uniting these children, some of them as old as 10 months, with their parents. Indeed, it is doubtful whether some children will ever be reunited with their parents.

But the intention was never to re-unite them but to send a message to would-be "trespassers" on American soil that they were not welcomed and they would be treated as inhumanely if they ever dared to cross the border. Jacob Soboroff, in his timely book *Separated: Inside an American Tragedy*, has done a lot of reporting on the American government's atrocities against children on the border. He has carefully documented the inhumane treatment of children; how they were placed in cages; the lack of social amenities at their disposal; the poor diet and the appalling psychological trauma to which they were subjected.

None of this seemed to matter to Trump. It was only when the nation was outraged by it that the policy of separation was ended. But the same callous elements remained. Today, children and adults in detainment centers on the border are under the threat of the covid-19 pandemic that has viciously impacted that region. There has been no indication from the Trump Administration of any compassion to these detainees in light of this threat. It is clear that Trump wants these unwelcomed visitors or aliens as members of the Republican Party likes to term them, to suffer. The infliction of pain seems to be Trump's chief weapon of deterrence. Thus, his wall should be electrified, there should be snake and alligator-infested moats, and it should have spikes.

Again, the Republican Party has remained devilishly silent in light of this sadistic approach to immigration. In the past, American policy has shown revulsion for immigrants of a particular race. For example, there was the internment of Japanese Americans in the Second World War and the rejection of Jewish refugees fleeing Germany and Europe from Hitler's tyranny. But we have not witnessed a more systematic and cruel treatment of immigrants as we have seen on the Southern border in the first three years of the Trump presidency.

There is clearly a cabal of operatives in the White House that is stoking the fire of hatred and bigotry towards immigrants. It is also clear that Trump is not in day to day control of his immigration policy. By his own admission he has ceded it to his chosen, trusted and loyal lieutenant, Stephen Miller, who has been very clinical in his use of the scalpels at his disposal.

The policy he is crafting for the administration is one which will severely curtail the flow of immigrants to this country. There is a clear preference for the immigrant of the Caucasian hue and for those with wealth. It is essentially a Eurocentric model of immigration which, if it succeeds, would issue into the balkanization of America and an increase in the xenophobic -prejudice against people from other countries-rhetoric in the country. Again, it is the fear of the shrinking of the European demography in the country, and the browning of America that drives the deepest fear in the hearts of those who preside over Trump's immigration policy. It is indeed the ultimate fear of white supremacy and of those who believe in

American racial purity. It is the essence of what is contained in the clarion call to make America great again.

On immigration alone, the voters should send a clear message to the administration that its conduct of immigration with all its racist, prejudicial and hate-filled characteristics, will not be rewarded. It should send the further message that a fairer system of immigration needs to be addressed which will result in comprehensive reform of a clearly broken system. The humbug is whether there is the political will and leadership that can command the moral fortitude to do the right and decent thing in enacting appropriate legislation that is fair and just and which can correct the problem well into the foreseeable future.

If there is anything that defines America as an exceptional nation it is simply its ability to accommodate people from every culture in the world into one melting pot of opportunity and prosperity. Today, that exceptionalism is under great strain because it is being presided over by a president whose native instincts pour scorn on others who are different from him. There will be no meaningful progress on the immigration issue of which most Americans can be proud. If he wins a second term, we may well see an America so shrunken and vitriolic that we may witness an exodus of Americans from America and not one in which people are beating a path to its shores. For this reason, the president should be sent a resounding message: "You're fired!"

# CHAPTER TWO

## DONALD J. TRUMP AND REPUBLICAN POLITICAL MALFEASANCE

*The greatest danger to American freedom is a government that ignores the Constitution*-Thomas Jefferson

In 2013, not long after Mitt Romney lost his presidential bid against President Obama, The Republican National Committee under the chairmanship of Reince Priebus, undertook a revision, or as some dubbed it, an "autopsy," of the reasons for the Republican Party's failure to advance in the election. Dubbed the "Growth and Opportunity Project," it was drafted by key strategists and communication experts in the party.

It was acknowledged that the party had reached an ideological cul-de-sac; that the party had failed to live up to its conservative values which had defined it over the years; that there was need for radical reform which would seriously consider the building of a "big tent" which would embrace a wider constituency in the party. As the report acknowledged:

*"We have become expert in how to provide ideological reinforcement to like-minded people, but devastatingly, we have lost the ability to be persuasive with, or welcoming to, those who do not agree with us on every issue."*

The report was intended to lay bare the Republican soul and to find new pathways for a party which many deemed had lost its way. Even a cursory reading of the report would reveal that it failed miserably to come up with any policies that would make a big tent out of the party. Conclusions focused more on the mechanisms of attaining future political victories such as having fewer presidential debates, shorter primary seasons and a reduction in the time taken to determine the presidential nominee for the party.

It was woefully short on any discussion of the deep-seated problems that faced the party, and on signature Republican policies such as taxes, gun control, same sex marriage and other bellwether issues that are basic to what is left of republican conservatism. Needless to say, the report did not receive a warm welcome from many important elements in the party, especially members of the Tea Party caucus. It hardly received the support that was worthy of the effort put into constructing it.

Today, seven years after the report was published, the Republican Party finds itself at the bleakest moment of its history. Many in and outside of the party saw this coming. Factionalism, petulance and the abandonment of key aspects of its conservative philosophy which gave it some respectability in the country-such as strong fiscal management and deficit restraint-have conspired to reduce the party to a mere vote-getting machine, characterized by an inner, rotting core.

It can safely be said that the party is no longer the party of Ronald Reagan, or stalwarts like George Bush Senior, Jack

Kemp or Bob Dole. Abraham Lincoln, the most illustrious member of the party ever, would not find a home in it today

In 2013, I wrote a book, *Beyond Petulance: Republican Politics and the Future of America*, in which I evaluated some of the reasons why the party lost the 2012 elections. Like the Priebus report, I was concerned about the shrinking base of the party, its general rejection of fiscal responsibility and embrace of deficit spending as seen in the Bush Junior tax cuts and the country's reckless adventure in Iraq. Equally jarring to the concerned observer of American politics was the party's continued exclusion of minority groups from key decision-making bodies and the creeping racism that was becoming far too entrenched in the party.

I saw a weakened and shrinking party that had lost its conservative core. As an immigrant I was interested in studying this phenomenon as I knew then, and know even more so today, that the country needs a strong Republican Party which can be an effective counter to the Democrats. That the strength of American democracy cannot be built on liberal ideals only, but on the energetic counterbalance of conservative ideals. The hope I had in writing that book is one that I still have, of a party which subscribes to values that could make the experiment called America worthwhile.

To my mind, the party had come to a bend in the road and it had taken a direction that could only take it farther on the path to decadence. I characterized the struggle then as a battle for the soul of the party. I was not the only person saying this. It had become a consensus, especially among the most cerebral elements of Republican politics.

Six years later we have come full circle. The petulance shown in the obstruction of the presidency of President Obama, coupled with the hardening of public discourse attendant upon the vitriol directed towards him, paved the road for an even more divided country. Furthermore, it opened the gate for the ascent of Donald J. Trump to the White House. Now we have truly gone beyond petulance to hard-fisted truculence and a kind of crass politics that the country has not seen before.

## Donald Trump and Republican Political Malfeasance

On November 4, 2016, Donald J. Trump was elected the 45th president of the United States. His election was a shock to most Americans and undoubtedly to the world at large. There was disbelief even within the Trump camp and perhaps with the candidate himself, that he had won. The country in recent memory had never seen a more belligerent candidate for the presidency. Although he lost the popular vote, he was able to squeak by with enough electoral college votes to become the most powerful person on planet earth.

Mr. Trump had telegraphed to the nation by word and deed that he was eminently unsuitable for the office to which he was elected. Repeatedly, in his personal life, he had demonstrated in dalliances with porn stars and by his own statement of what he would do to the female genitalia, that he had serious moral lapses that the country should be wary of. As a businessman he had filed bankruptcy repeatedly to get out from under his debts. In saner days in American politics, this is not the person you would want to make appointments to the Federal Reserve, the Treasury department and other agencies that need strong, judicial and fiduciary oversight. There were suspicions regarding his business dealings, both domestically and internationally, about which the country should have been more mindful in hiring him for the job.

From what could be gleaned from the candidate's personal and business résumé, he was not the kind of person who would be asked to serve as chairman or chief executive officer of any of America's leading corporations. It is doubtful that with his record he could have made it to any second or third tier corporation. If he was dispassionately evaluated, it is doubtful that he could be appointed to run a local Boys Scout organization. Yet, here he was elected to be the CEO of America's destiny, if not the world's.

Alas, many in his base saw him as a savvy businessman, a television star to boot, who they really believed would "make America great again", the slogan that helped to catapult him to office. For many in his base, Trump could do no wrong, a sentiment which made Trump comfortable enough to make the statement that he could shoot a man on Fifth Avenue in New York and they would still vote for him. And voted for him they did, notwithstanding his intellectual deficits, his eminent unfitness for office, and his delusions of grandeur as to what he could accomplish. Giving inordinate power such as the presidency of the United States to such a person, was tantamount to giving a child a grenade with the pin pulled out.

He has not dropped it yet, but many have lived in fear wondering when he might. Mr. Trump set the tone for the kind of president he would become from his inaugural address in January, 2020. He spoke inelegantly of the carnage that America had become largely under President Obama and of how he would restore prosperity to America. In his first 100 days in office, he signed a slew of Executive Orders, a practice for which he had castigated President Obama for presidential overreach. To my memory, no president has signed in their first term the number of Executive Orders than Trump has done so far in his. A careful study may reveal that neither has any in two terms in office. And he still has some time to go. If he loses the election, I can foresee between November 4, 2020 and January 20, 2021, what I would describe as executive orders on steroids, as he tries to implement pet policies before he leaves the White House. This may sound farfetched, but we should remember that with the Donald, nothing can be assumed. His has been the unprecedented presidency.

From the very start it was clear how he intended to govern. In many conversations I said to people that whatever Mr. Trump could do he would do. Over his nearly four years in office, he has demonstrated repeatedly by word and action that he would not be constrained by any ethical consideration in how he conducted the office. Moral scruples in decision-making was anathema to him. We saw this in his baby-snatching policy on the Southern border.

His approach to the office was fundamentally what it has always been for Mr. Trump: transactional, the making of the deal and what personal benefits he could derive from it. The immorality of an action-such as the suffering that many Americans would undergo if he killed the Affordable Care Act (ACA) and his lying about pre-existing conditions, did not deter him as long as he was convinced of the legality of his actions. Even when the courts ruled against the legality of an action, he was reticent to change course.

You see, Mr. Trump has behaved as if he is the veritable dean of lawsuits. Not only has he been sued several times by others, but he himself has initiated many lawsuits over his long career. He has inevitably carried this mentality into the presidency as is evidenced in the number of lawsuits proffered against him or entered into on his behalf. There is nothing wrong with being sued or suing someone. The courts exist to dispense fair justice and remain avenues for persons who fail to settle disputes among themselves.

Lawsuits do not necessarily disqualify one from being president. But when there is such a plethora of them that bear your name, there has to be something concerning about your ability or willingness to negotiate and settle disputes in which you are involved. It says something about your powers of negotiation, if not humility in accepting where you may be wrong and making a decision to go in a decisively new direction. When you so frequently fail to walk this path, it should be sufficient to at least give a voter pause as to whether you have the kind of temperament required to do as important a job as the president of the United States.

Before he ascended to the high office he had telegraphed to the American people and the world that he lacked this judicial temperament to do a good job as President. Americans expect their presidents to behave with a certain decorum in office. They do not expect them to be saints, great moralists or shrinking violets. Indeed, some have shown grievous moral lapses and character flaws which might have disqualified them from becoming president. In Mr. Trump, many of these challenges were present, but he was elected nonetheless, beating his many primary contenders to become the nominee for his party and then going on to win the presidency.

Despite his obvious characterological flaws and his often-disgusting in-your-face tweeting behavior, people just resigned themselves to the Trump presidency, hoping that the demands of the office would somehow soften and refine him. I, too, to my utmost embarrassment, and against my wife's better judgment, harbored these sentiments. In doing so I ignored the sage advice of the great Maya Angelou when she said: "When someone shows you who they are, believe them the first time." I believed he would at least try to behave like the leader of the free world.

If Americans had believed Trump the first time as Angelou advised, he might not have been elected president. But here we are today. Four years into his first term Trump has left no doubt as to the veracity of Angelou's statement. Having grown accustomed to fairly smooth transitions of administrations, Americans were appalled at the shambolic and chaotic nature of the Trump process. With the exception of a few appointments, Trump, always mindful of his own agenda which often superseded that of the nation's, appointed people to offices in his Cabinet and the White House whom he knew would do his bidding.

Within two years some of those appointees had either resigned or had been summarily and unceremoniously fired by Mr. Trump. His first three years saw the greatest turnover in Cabinet level personnel that we have witnessed in American government in recent memory. Those who left undoubtedly failed to fit into his transactional grid, or to toe the line, or were simply too incompetent to have been appointed in the first place. Some eliminated themselves by their own bad behavior in office while others, including his Secretary of State Rex Tillerson, were fired by a tweet.

Mr. Trump's desire to do things his own way without any opposition can be seen in the number of acting appointees he has in his administration. According to Fortune Magazine, Mr. Trump has had no less than 28 acting Cabinet secretaries. This is more than the 27 that served under president Clinton in his eight years in office and 23 in the course of the Obama administration (*All the Acting Heads of Trump's Presidency,* **Natasha Bach, Fortune Magazine, November 27, 2019**).

There is nothing unusual, unethical or even illegal in having acting appointments in government, but the rapid turnover of personnel as is happening in the Trump administration speaks volumes to the chaotic nature of the way he has chosen to govern. Whenever he could circumvent the senatorial advice and consent process, he relished in doing so. This is when he could appoint persons that fit into his transactional mindset and put in train what he wanted to get done. He left no doubt that he demanded personal loyalty from his appointees which meant that they were serving him, and not with him, to advance the best interests of the American people.

Although it is known that presidential appointees serve at the president's pleasure, Mr. Trump carried this principle to its most callous extremes at times simply on the basis that he had the power to do so. Remember that anything he could do, he would do. He seldomly fired people himself, and if he did it was under the blanket of his twitter finger. He would use surrogates to carry out his desires which is what apparently happened in the firing of former FBI Deputy Director, Andrew McCabe, by Attorney General Jeff Sessions. This occurred two days before McCabe was set to retire. As it turned out the action was one of utmost cruelty as it would cost a significant portion of his retirement benefits.

The summary dismissal of personnel has a daunting effect on those who would want to do their work to the best of their abilities and in the service of their country. If they have to please a boss who will not hesitate to fire them, this creates an environment of intimidation and anxiety for many workers. A policy of intimidation cauterizes any sense of patriotic duty that these workers may have. While they are mindful of doing their work well, they also realize that the job provides them a livelihood. Many are not able to just pick up and leave. Those who are able to leave in disgust as many have done.

This speaks to the heart of governance and how well one understands how the federal apparatus of government works. Mr. Trump has proven himself incurious in understanding this as can be seen in the toxic relationship he has with the Congress. The president fundamentally resents any kind of oversight, especially from the Congress, a co-equal branch of government which has constitutional responsibility to exercise oversight over the Executive branch. Mr. Trump does not want to have anybody peering over his shoulders or telling him that his pet agendas will not be accommodated or need to be revised. He will throw a tantrum or rather a "tantrump," if he should be denied, by putting up all kinds of obstacles in the way of investigators. Whenever he can obstruct such oversight, he does so. He does not seem to be concerned about a fair or just outcome to any process that would help the American people. His obsession is always with how he can benefit personally from any such engagement.

The net result of all this has been chaos and tension in the White House and the nation at large. Americans in recent memory have never witnessed such a chaotic start to a new administration. Neither have they seen a president given to such intemperate outbursts, name calling of opponents, irascibility and petulance in getting his way, especially against perceived enemies. All of this has contributed significantly to the chaotic nature of his administration. Mr. Trump seems to have embraced chaos as an integral aspect of political governance. One would have to be very clueless to believe that any of the above will change if he is given another four years in office. But I will leave that discussion for later.

Chaos is not the only word that has gained currency in describing Trump's presidency. Another is "unprecedented." Trump's time in office can truly be described as the "unprecedented presidency." I have never heard the word used more frequently to describe a presidential administration. What lies behind the phrase is the shock at the extreme to which Mr. Trump is willing to stretch the boundaries of the powers that he has or believes he has. It speaks to his willingness to ride roughshod over traditions and conventions that Americans consider almost sacred; to kick aside anything that did not comport with his transactional approach to doing things; his almost pathological mendacity in denying things that are so patently true; his trivial regard for the rule of law and his lack of curiosity in understanding the danger that he might expose the country to. A case in point is the deference he has given to Russia in light of that president's clear interference in the electoral affairs of America.

Any one of these could be fertile ground for the impeachment of any president. But Mr. Trump does them with such dizzying frequency that he is reconstructing the presidency in such a radical and badly transformative way that people become exhausted and may very well consider his behavior part of the new normal of governance. This is the real danger. What may be considered gentlemanly agreements can be easily pushed aside by a president who clearly harbors autocratic aspirations.

If there is one thing that should be learnt from all this, it is that some of these conventions and traditions that were once considered sacrosanct, will now have to be enshrined in law. They can no longer be taken for granted. When they are captured in law, they can become more airtight and be a firewall to any future president who would not subscribe to them or who believes he or she should not be constrained by them. We should not believe for one moment that among the over 300 million Americans, there are not potential demagogues among them who harbor these machinations. As the 19th century British politician, Lord Acton, advised us, power tends to corrupt and absolute power corrupts absolutely. We may yet thank Mr. Trump for alerting us to the dangers of the absolute corruption of power.

So, Mr. Trump rode into Washington from his glitzy Trump Tower in New York to the people's house, the White House, with a solid commitment he made to his followers to shake up Washington, or as he put it, to drain the swamp. Instead, into the fourth year of his presidency, almost 60 percent of Americans are convinced that he has merely increased the toxicity of the swamp. Some may even say that he is the commander in chief of the swamp. as he seems to have elevated hatred and bigotry to social principles. Washington is perhaps more divided today than it has ever been. In Congress, the division and social hostility it has spawned, is so palpable that many citizens have simply withdrawn from the political process.

Today, the Republican Party has come full circle to a place of ennui. When Mr. Trump just went into office, I noted that his elevation to the presidency was just an aberration. I have heard Joe Biden with a similar analysis. But I have revised my opinion, for when I look at what the Republican Party has become, I am now convinced more than ever that Mr. Trump is the natural culmination of what the party is today. The party had been moving inexorably over the past 20 years to its present status. Its abandonment of conservative values which accelerated under Bush the Younger, picked up steam in its rabid, petulant and often childish opposition to the policies of President Obama. These have now borne sour grapes under Mr. Trump.

It is not clear what Republicans believe in today. It has become shrunken and lacking in any cogent philosophy or ideas of what can move the country forward. This is so because it has become completely beholden to Mr. Trump. A man who believes in his own invincibility and a grandiose sense of his almost superhuman abilities, owns the party.

His consistently high favorability rating in the party above the 90-percentile range, tells the story. The party is now firmly his and it is amazing how the Grand Old Party and its future can be so firmly tethered to a man whom well-placed therapists and psychoanalysts seem to think have a serious narcissistic personality challenge and who, by his words and actions, has not disavowed these assessments. Even the man in the street is convinced that there is some truth to these evaluations, though there are still many who view these traits as a position of strength.

The big tent idea once paraded by real conservatives in the party is no more. Today it has just been reduced to a shriveled base of what I would describe as the calcified. I have coined the term "political calcification" to describe those in the base who have become so wedded to the philosophies of a political leader that they have become bewitchingly loyal to him or her. In broader political scientific terms, political calcification is the process by which people become so hardened to a political ideology that they will defend this with a fierce loyalty even if it goes against their best interests. It betrays a cultic fealty to the political leader.

This may amaze those who are looking in from the outside. In the case of Mr. Trump, they may be amazed at the extent to which a stubborn one-third remains so loyal to him that they will defend his every word and action. They are more than diehards of the party. Their loyalty to this one person is almost messianic and they could not care less about what the wider party thinks.

It is this calcified group that Mr. Trump is relying on to win in November. It is to them that his bigoted and racist statements are addressed; the ones he relies on to defend the streets against the marauding democratic socialists and anarchists; to not wear masks in the midst of a pandemic, and a host of other behavior that defines their loyalty to a messianic leader.

Whatever is left of mainline republicanism cannot understand this segment of the party, because Mr. Trump has so completely taken it over. Many, in embarrassment, have become supinely silent and have simply resigned themselves and their political future to this shrinking base. They may grumble in the halls and corridors of Congress or in their congressional offices, but they do not have the temerity to speak out. They are essentially political amoeba lacking the backbone to stand up for what they really believe, backing instead a president that they know in their heart represents a grave danger to the country.

Wittingly or unwittingly, they are now beholden to Mr. Trump and his base. And the base is Trump's, not the party's. So, leading Republicans like Mitch McConnell, Marco Rubio, Lindsay Graham and others have been politically emasculated. By their supine acceptance of Trump's behavior, they too are a danger to the future of America. I can understand one's fidelity to a political party, but I am befuddled as to how well-meaning men and women who make it to what was once considered the most deliberative body on earth, the US Senate, can defend with such fierce loyalty, political thinking and action that is so much against their own best interests, the health and livelihood of the people they represent, and the constitution they have sworn to protect and defend. In no other area has this fawning fealty to Trumpism been more evident, than in the impeachment of Donald J. Trump, the 45th president of the United States, to which I will now turn.

## Impeachment of Donald J. Trump

When Mr. Trump started his presidency there are two things I said repeatedly to friends, family members and those who would care to listen. I have already referred to one of these, that anything Trump could do he would do. The other was that the time would come when he would stub his toe against the constitution in such a serious way that he may have to be removed from office. I made this assertion based on my belief that Trump's blatant disregard for the rule of law, his notion that he alone could fix things, and his willingness to shove aside conventions that had made the presidency respectable, would one day cause him to face impeachment. Some in Congress, including the chairwoman of the House Finance Committee, Mrs. Maxine Waters, had already called for his impeachment.

Even though there were compelling evidence that he should be impeached as was evident in the Mueller report into the president's conduct regarding Russian interference in the 2016 election, the Speaker of the House, Nancy Pelosi, balked. Not long after, a whistleblower complained about the content of a conversation that Trump had had with the newly elected young president of the Ukraine, Volodymyr Zelensky.

This blew the impeachment enquiry wide open. True to his transactional nature and seeing the peril that faced his presidency, Trump used all the power at his disposal to frustrate the process. He refused to let important witnesses testify in the proceedings. He refused to turn over important documents and thus obstructed the Congress in its pursuit of essential information germane to the investigation.

After weighing all the evidence it could muster from interested parties who testified on the Hill, Pelosi and the Congress, dominated by Democrats, preferred articles of impeachment against the 45th president of The United States, Donald John Trump. Trump thus became the fourth president in American history to have impeachment articles preferred against him and the third to be impeached in history, though the Senate failed in getting the votes necessary to remove him form office.

What was instructive during the impeachment proceedings in the Senate was the extent to which Republicans were willing to defend Trump. With the exception of Senator Mitt Romney who saw the danger that Trump represented to the Republic, the remaining senators all voted not to impeach. At the very rudimentary level, they refused to have witnesses called to testify and joined with Mr. Trump to ensure that he did not have the fair trial to which he was entitled. Furthermore, it cheated the public of fairly participating in the process as it was not able to hear or see evidence by which it could make its own determination in a democratic republic. None of this seemed important to the Republicans who petulantly, against all common-sense, was determined in their endeavor to have Mr. Trump remain in office, no matter what. Such testimonies might have elicited a trove of evidence so compelling that even the most recalcitrant Republican senator would have found it difficult not to have voted to impeach. The best default position for them was to suppress the evidence.

As it turned out, having voted for him to remain in office, they became witting or unwitting accomplices in any dastardly action that Mr. Trump would henceforth carry out as president. They decided to dine with him and they did so with short spoons. They were now unwitting allies to any skullduggery that would inform his post-impeachment behavior in office. And Trump has not disappointed. Flushed with what he perceived as victory, he moved to reward some of his greatest loyalists and defenders such as Mark Meadows, congressional representative for North Carolina's 11th congressional district. He was elevated to the White House as Trump's Chief of Staff.

Since impeachment, Trump's behavior in office has shocked the sensibilities of the nation. His autocratic, and some would argue fascist, sensibilities were on display when he seemed to countenance the teargassing of innocent protesters at a park in downtown Washington DC. Ostensibly, this was to allow the president a photo opportunity with Bible in hand before the St. John's Episcopal church. Since then a veritable "goon" squad has emerged from the Department of Homeland Security under the guise of defending federal buildings in areas where protesters gather in large numbers to protest racial injustice. Some of these protests have been suppressed with violence, largely from militia groups that have inserted themselves in these protests to spread mayhem. Mr. Trump has seen these protests as a way of cementing himself in the minds of his followers that he is the law and order president and Mr. Biden as a violent anarchist.

From all appearances, he seems to have stepped up his efforts to bend a too willing Attorney General, William Barr, to do his bidding. Contrary to accepted norms and practice, and in the thinking of many social and political commentators, the Attorney General has acted more like the President's lawyer than the impartial chief law enforcer whose job is to protect the interests of the United States. What message was the country's attorney general sending by walking with the president after a controversial teargassing of legitimate protesters? Unfortunately, the Chairman of the Joint Chiefs of Staff, General Mark Milley, was also present, an action for which he later apologized to the nation. We are yet to hear an apology from Mr. Barr.

In recent memory the country has not seen a set of senators more willing to give succor to the most egregious excesses of a president. To a great extent they have behaved as an extension of the Executive, taking their cues from the White House on important legislation. They have failed to realize that constitutionally they are a co-equal branch of government and do not have to be beholden to a president.

They have failed to upbraid the president when he intimidated or otherwise suppressed innocent protesters. Their silence has been deafening in light of the apparent efforts of the president to destabilize the work of the United States Post Office in the run up to the elections in November 3. At the time of writing over 200,000 people have died from Covid-19 with close to seven million infected. In the light of this rising existential threat, we are yet to see any attempt by the Republicans to criticize the president or even to offer any strategic solution as to the way forward.

In the midst of the raging pandemic, the president conducts political rallies in indoor settings where thousands of people are assembled, many of them not wearing masks. This is often in contravention of regulations instituted by local authorities to prevent the spread of the virus. But the president brushes these aside and simply does not seem to care. He admitted to Bob Woodward, the quintessential American journalist, that he knew from very early that the virus is dangerous and is easily transmitted, yet he goes about in large crowds without wearing a mask. And there is not even a voice from the Republican amoebas in Congress to even urge the president to exercise caution and due care or to reprimand him for his reckless disregard for the safety if citizens.

There are important bills that have been sent by the House of Representatives to the senate that are yet to be acted on. They have failed to push back against Trump's roll back of environmental regulations which will further climate change and the existential danger we all face.

When the report came out from the intelligence agencies that Russian president Putin had placed a bounty on the heads of US soldiers in Afghanistan, there was some grumbling of dissatisfaction from some senators, but no concerted effort to help the president craft a credible response to this threat, perceived or otherwise.

Mr. Trump is alleged to have spoken disparagingly of servicemen and women who have fought and died in the service of their country. He has reportedly called them 'losers" and "suckers." To the extent that this true it would be quite pathetic for it would be coming from a man who got several deferments from serving in the armed forces. Furthermore, as Commander in chief of the armed forces, it would be coming from a person who should be respectful of the service and sacrifice of those who put their lives on the line for the country he is privileged to be president of.

There is so much more that could be mentioned here, but the picture is clear. Under President Trump, we are not just faced with a battle for the soul of the Republican Party, but for the sustenance of the basic elements of decency in public life that have served the country well and without which it can only descend into a vortex of hatred and instability. And there is more that can come from an irascible president who is only concerned about perpetuating himself in power, no matter the winds of immorality which fan his passions. He and the Republican Party he leads have squandered any sense of credibility that should allow them to continue to preside over people's lives. Collectively, on November 3, 2020, the people of America who still believe in the viability of the great experiment that the country is, should send a resounding message to the president: "You're fired!"

# CHAPTER THREE

## THE CASE AGAINST DONALD TRUMP

### PART ONE- The Covid-19 Pandemic

*"To be honest with you, I wanted to always play it down. I still like playing it down, because I don't want to create panic."* (President Trump's taped statement to journalist Bob Woodward about the coronavirus pandemic).

Senator Kamala Harris, vice-presidential nominee for the Democratic ticket, said it best that the case against Trump and his administration is open and shut. Her prosecutorial judgment in this matter can hardly be questioned. In no area is this case most apparent than that of the president's handling of the coronavirus pandemic, and to that I will now turn.

His lack of empathy for suffering Americans without healthcare has filled many with dread as Trump attempts through the Supreme Court to remove any remaining vestige of the Affordable Care Act (ACA) derisively called Obamacare by some, but refreshingly by others, in the midst of the worst health crisis to hit this country in 100 years.

When the coronavirus landed in America, it could not have found a more fertile soil for infectious spread in a divided nation. As it was to prove, the deep social, economic and political divisions in the country, coupled with the incompetent leadership of a hubristic president, were to combine to make America an embarrassment to the world.

Let us be clear: President Trump did not introduce the virus to America, but his incompetent leadership of the crisis seen in the lethargic federal response to it, were primary factors for its spread throughout the country and the ongoing failure to bring it under control.

From the very beginning, the president labelled his approach to the virus as a war against an invisible enemy. But he failed to bring any comprehensive and strategic measures to the conflict worthy of a Commander in Chief. He failed to use the vast resources of the richest country on earth to strike a decisive blow against the virus. There was no central command, no organized federal response. Instead what we had was a hodge-podge of policies evidenced by his fobbing off responsibility to fight the virus to the states.

This created confusion as states had to compete with each other for the scarce personal protective equipment that first responders required to protect themselves and the many patients who were piling up in the hospitals. Robust testing and the necessary contact tracing to contain community spread of the virus was lethargic, if not non-existent in vast swathes of the country. This continues to be the case as there is no federally, organized approach.

It was only after the virus started to spread rapidly through the population, and states like California and New York were being overwhelmed by it, having been forced to initiate lockdown procedures, that the president initiated a

White House task force to fight the virus. We have seen how that has worked out. By the end of May when he forced the re-opening of the economy, the president's task force was virtually non-existent.

In any event, it had started to fade in the minds of most Americans as people saw from early that it had descended into the theatrics of a reality television show starring one man: Donald Trump. It had lost its credibility because its chief spokesperson, the President, was toting snake oil cures such as hydroxychloroquine and disinfectants as possible treatment modalities.

With his eyes firmly fixed on November 3 and the polls showing him trailing his opponent, Trump made the calculation from the very beginning that whatever approach he took must be in tune with his election prospects in November. Nothing else seemed to matter. Not the hundreds of people who were dying daily nor the thousands who were battling for their lives in the hospitals.

There was hardly any empathy for those who died nor for the families, friends or colleagues of the dead. At his briefings he failed repeatedly to show the nation that he was even aware of these statistics. Having made himself and not the virus the subject, the president reasoned that rising cases of the affected would make him look bad. Thus, it was necessary to keep the numbers down so that it would not reflect badly on his handling of it.

At every gathering where he could get a listening ear, he repeated the false line that rising cases of infection throughout the country were a result of the amount of testing that was being done. He failed to see that what the tests were capturing was the extent to which the virus was spreading throughout the country. The tests were merely revealing the infection rates and were not themselves causing the virus to spread. So, at a rally in Tulsa, Oklahoma Trump, in true braggadocio style, trumpeted to his audience that he told his people to slow the testing down. "When you do testing to that extent," he told his audience of supporters, most of whom were not wearing masks, "You're going to find more cases. So, I said to my people, 'Slow the testing down, please.'"

In another attempt to suppress information on the virus, Trump's White House decided to bypass the Center for Disease Control (CDC) by re-routing data on infections and deaths from hospitals from that body. The data were temporarily removed from their website but restored after howls of protest. The intention here was clear: to suppress or otherwise sanitize the negative news going out on the pandemic so it would not look too bad on the administration and its inept handling of the pandemic.

Contrary to the president's wish for the magical disappearance of the virus, it has continued its deadly trek throughout the country. The re-opening of the economy and holiday events such as Memorial Day and Independence celebrations, gave Americans the reprieve they wanted or needed to go outdoors and exhale, after having been locked in their homes for almost two months. Many were suffering from "cabin fever" and there were signs of mental distress among some people. Also, small businesses were beginning to feel the pinch of the lockdown.

As the measures were relaxed, many breathed the open air with great relish, but they were also breathing in the virus that had not disappeared but was merely waiting for willing bodies to infect. In June and July various hotspots emerged in the country and soon proved problematic with rising cases of daily infections in large states such as Florida and Texas.

Yet, with this continuing problem the president failed to even appeal to people to wear masks. Repeatedly, the scientists on his re-started task force appealed to people to wear masks, but the president steadfastly refused to wear one himself. He only did so on a few occasions when he had to.

The non-wearing of masks has become a symbol of defiance and even more so a statement of political defiance. It is a phenomenon that many within the country and around the world have found it difficult to fathom. They cannot understand how such a basic and simple requirement for health in the midst of a pandemic should be the subject of so much discussion and division.

While the non-wearing of masks is predominantly political, it is not necessarily so for some people who regard it a matter of the freedoms they enjoy under the constitution. You may not agree with them, especially in light of a pandemic, but it is a deeply held view that can have fatal consequences for themselves and others around them.

In any event, defiance has been an essential aspect of the American spirit to be free. It can be seen in the revolutionary war for independence where the Boston Tea Party on December 16, 1773 was the ultimate act of defiance by the colonists against taxation without representation under an autocratic monarchy.

The spirit of defiance was also evident in the Civil Rights Movement where black Americans by non-violent protests asserted their basic human rights in an oppressive white society. Martin Luther King who led the movement was himself profoundly influenced by Mahatma Gandhi whose defiance of the British in various non-violent protests won independence for India.

Latterly, defiance has become embedded in the Black Lives Matter movement, especially since the death of George Floyd. Despite a raging pandemic, thousands of citizens-black, brown, white and Asian-took to the streets throughout the country to protest against police brutality against blacks, the resurgence of white supremacy, and systemic racial injustice that has impoverished people of color for too long in this society.

There is nothing wrong with having a defiant spirit. I believe it is an essential part of who we are as human beings. It was built in us for self-preservation. While it is an important part of what America is, I can see how it can tend for good or for evil. I believe not wearing a mask because you are a member of a political party in the midst of a raging pandemic that demands that you wear one, is not only insensitive to what should be one's concern for the neighbor, but is illogical, nonsensical and lacking in essential common sense.

So, the blame for Americans not wearing masks cannot be placed at the feet of the president altogether. He might have given voice and legitimacy to this foolish, if not evil, defiance, but Americans bear personal responsibility for their own defiance here. It has been well attested that wearing masks in this time of COVID-19 crisis does save lives. It is a simple, though uncomfortable exercise, which is one of the most effective ways in containing the spread of the virus and helping all of us to return to some semblance of normality in our lives.

But normality will not return anytime soon, even if we should find a treatment or get an effective vaccine against the virus. Whether we are in a second wave or seeing continuing spikes in the first wave, the country is still in a serious danger zone. At the time of writing, America has over six million confirmed cases of the virus, with close to 200,000 deaths. The country is still losing over 1,000 Americans to the virus daily. America has over one quarter of the world's infection cases.

Yet, despite these tragic statistics, there is still not a nationally coordinated effort from the federal level of government to fight the disease. The president is still pushing states to re-open, especially for children to go back to school. The president's task force as presently constituted is almost a sham. It is distinguished only by its inability to give any assurance to the country that they are on top of the disease. A president who seeks to be praised that he is doing a good job (when he isn't) and who rants that one of the scientists on his task force gets more accolades than he does, is not one who can be trusted to do all that he can to subdue the virus. In his own words, "It is what it is."

And winter is coming when the seasonal flu virus will be joining hands with first cousin Covid-19 to make our lives miserable. The Director of the Center for Disease Control (CDC), Dr. Robert Redfield, has lamented that with the present rate of spread, we may be in for the worst fall season of our lifetimes. What about it being the worst winter?

What is clear is that we never had to be where we are today, helpless and almost impotent to get this disease under control. History will not be kind to the Trump administration and the Republican Party by extension, for how they have responded to this crisis. The party controls both the Executive (the presidency) and the Senate. Mitch McConnell, Leader of the senate, and other Republican senators have been very silent in the face of the president's many egregious remarks on the virus and the general lack of effective response to it. Many in the party have resisted the wearing of masks, yet there has not been any serious pushback from prominent members of the party. They bend to Mr. Trump's wishes even when they know deep down that yielding is against their own consciences and best interests.

President Trump's fatal mistake is that from the beginning he tried to spin information about the virus to get a narrative that would fit neatly into his political agenda. But this has not worked. In fact, his inept and uncompassionate handling of the virus, sautéed with putrid theatrics about it, has caused many Americans to be so turned off from him that they no longer listen to what he has to say.

If I were a betting man, I would wager that over 50 percent of the American people no longer listen to him. They either turn off their televisions, turn to another channel, or as one man told me, be tempted to throw a brick at it, whenever the president is making a speech about the virus. They do not expect him to talk the truth and don't believe what he is telling them. He grates on their nerves. A recent CNN poll asserted that 68 percent of the people are embarrassed at how the country's leaders has handled the virus.

If my assumption is right that over 50 percent no longer listen to him, then this is as pathetic as it is dangerous. It is pathetic when over 50 percent of a people no longer care for what their leader is telling them. It is also dangerous in that a great deal of evil can develop in governance when there is a serious disconnect between the governed and their governors. They are turned off because they know that whenever the president speaks, he is largely speaking to his base and not to them. Trump's delusions may allow him to think that he is getting through to people, but he is speaking to an ever-shrinking minority in this country. From focus group interactions with Republicans or those who voted for him in 2016, one can see that he is even losing some who voted for him.

The president's inept handling of the virus coupled with his obscuring the truth about it about it to serve political ends, and his pursuit of quirky cures, have caused immense suffering and hardships in the country. I believe that there is a growing tsunami of resentment that is building up against the him among those who have lost loved ones, friends and colleagues to the virus. In fact, it is more than resentment; it is a seething anger for what is perceived as the needless loss of their loved ones.

While they will not blame him for introducing the virus to America, they will certainly do so for his incompetent handling of the crisis especially at its most basic, rudimentary level. They will blame him for not taking the pandemic seriously from the start, even though, by his taped admission to journalist Bob Woodward, he knew that it was easily transmissible and dangerous. They will not forgive him for his clear politicization of the issue seen in him not insisting on a national mask wearing policy; for his many untruths about the statistics on rising infections and deaths and the obvious marketing of snake-oil cures for the virus. Most importantly, they will blame him for his lack of empathy for the suffering; for his treating the dead as mere statistics as characterized in his most indelicate and insensitive remark to a journalist when asked about the thousands that have died that "It is what it is."

Occasionally, those who have lost loved ones vent their anger in the media, but it is largely a silent majority who have embraced their pain quietly but waiting patiently for the day when they will register that anger tangibly in the ballot box. I believe that the full brunt of their revulsion will be felt on November 3. The lived experiences of people cannot be spun and neither should they be trivialized. People know what they are going though and no amount of denying it will change the picture.

What I am not certain of is the extent to which this quiet anger is captured in the polls. The exponential effects of this disaffection cannot be minimized. Let's do some math here. If by the end of October 220,000 Americans should have died from the virus, you are talking about that amount of families. If there are four members to an immediate family, this would be 880,000 disaffected and angry people, not counting other family members and acquaintances, friends, work colleagues and members of churches and fraternity organizations of those who have died. The exponential effect of this across the country could be staggering. Whatever the mathematical outcomes, it is clear to me that what I am calling this seething, quiet minority, will be a further nail in the political coffin of Donald Trump. On November 3, it may prove to be his worst nightmare.

And this seething anger does not even account for the many people who have lost their jobs and businesses. The failure of the administration to contain the virus has postponed any robust re-opening of the economy. The basic proposition that there can be no robust re-opening of the economy without a robust containment of the virus has been lost on the administration. The net effect of this blind sidedness is the uncertainty that faces many small businesses, and the appalling suffering of many who were already living from paycheck to paycheck. Combine this with the bereaved noted above and one can see that this cannot spell well for the president on November 3.

There is no doubt that Mr. Trump has long lost any moral ground he may have occupied on this pandemic. As the great fixer-in-chief he came to the people as the one who could "fix things." He even boasted that when it came to military engagements, he knew more than the generals. This, from a man who when his country needed him, filed for deferment from military service.

But he has failed as a Commander in Chief to deal resolutely with the defining crisis of our times. When the history of this period is written, it will record a sad indictment of Trump and the impotent political party he leads for making a proud nation a pitiful embarrassment to the world. For this we should all weep.

## Terminating the Affordable Care Act (Obamacare)

Perhaps one of the most egregious, unconscionable and heartless actions on the part of the president, aided and abetted by the Republican party which he leads, obviously with an iron hand, is the desperation to have the Supreme Court end the Affordable Care Act (ACA). We should all weep when we consider the implications of this dastardly action. The ACA provides health insurance for millions of Americans who would not otherwise have any. In the midst of a pandemic, when the number of people without insurance has grown exponentially because they have lost their jobs, millions more will be hurt. Yet, with Republican quiescence, Mr. Trump reaffirmed his intention to end the law when his Justice department joined briefs with 20 Republican-controlled states before the Supreme Court.

The Republican Party has made no secret of their intention to end the Affordable Care Act. They have tried repeatedly to do so and almost succeeded had it not been for the patriotic and compassionate John McCain of blessed memory, who, by only one motion of his thumb pointing downward, ended his party's predatory attack on the act.

There should be no illusion as to the enormous difficulties that terminating Obamacare would mean for millions of Americans. Immediately it would end the provision that Americans cannot be denied health insurance because they have a pre-existing condition. This would be a huge blow in the face of the pandemic since many Americans, including younger ones, many of whom would no longer be able to stay on their parent's health insurance, could be denied coverage. COVID-19 would now become a pre-existing condition.

This is so despite the president's mendacious attempts to say otherwise. Neither he nor the Republican Party has any viable plan to come up with a health insurance policy anytime soon. Furthermore, millions of Americans who have benefitted from the Act's Medicaid provisions would no longer do so if it should be ended. It is estimated that over 15 million Americans have been added to the Medicaid rolls since the Act was enacted.

What is pathetic is the cavalier way the Republican Party is treating people's health. In its cultic fealty to the president and its attempt to erase President Obama's signature achievement in office, it cannot see the incalculable harm removing the Act would have on people's lives. They have not come up with a viable replacement in ten years and you can be certain they will not do so in two months. What we see playing out before us is an unconscionable and reckless disregard for the health of the American people. It is all about re-electing the president. Never mind the millions of people who will suffer as a result.

But there is just one sliver of hope in all this that may save the ACA: Chief Justice John Roberts. He singlehandedly saved it before and I can see him once again coming to the rescue and adding the vote that will save the act. If there is any smidgen of compassion left in the hearts of the conservative justices on the court, I can see this residing more prominently in the heart of Chief Justice Roberts. Too many people will be hurt needlessly by the Republican's heartless move at a time when they are fighting to keep alive in the middle of a pandemic.

Apart from his outlandish statements and lack of empathy, one of the most remarkable things about Mr. Trump's abysmal failure in combating the virus, is his and his team's shortsightedness in not recognizing how they could have turned the crisis to their political advantage. Eminent common sense would dictate that had he gone the other way and truly put up a sensible and reasonable fight against the virus as so many countries had done, that his political stocks could have been different. If he had just used effectively the full powers of the federal government that are given to a president in the time of a national emergency, by this time he would have given Biden more than a political headache to deal with.

But through his self-centered lens, he failed to recognize the simple equation that if the virus is not contained, the economy on which he pins so much hope for re-election, will not be opened in time to give him a fighting chance. In fact, Trump faces the grim realization that time is not his best friend. He is racing against the political clock. As it ticks so does his desperation meter.

He dismally failed to recognize that you cannot manipulate a virus, an invisible enemy, to do your political bidding, no matter how powerful a president you may think you are. The virus bends to no one's agenda. That is the lesson we have been forced to learn at tremendous cost to the country. On this history will not be kind to the 45th president of the United States.

Also, it will not be kind to those who have supported the president in his lying about the virus. I have already mentioned his lackeys in the party, but there is one media institution that merits special attention. At the start of the pandemic in America, the misinformation coming from analysts at the Fox News Network has been well documented. The network seemed committed to become a close ally of the president in denying the science about the virus and spinning information on its spread. Generally, they sold the idea that it should not be taken seriously suggesting at times that it could be compared to the common flu. They gave credence to the quack remedies that he touted and refused to push back vigorously against some of Trump's more egregious statements such as when he talked about using disinfectants as a possible cure.

The hypocrisy of the Fox propagandists was exposed in that while they were pushing their false narrative about the virus, they were ensuring that they kept themselves safe by abiding by the CDC protocols to wear masks, physically distant themselves, use hand sanitizers, wash hands, and avoid large gatherings. Like other media personnel, they observed stay at home protocols and did their work from there. If the virus was not one to be taken seriously, why even bother to observe any protocol at all?

A far more grievous question though, is how many people might have died because they bought into the misinformation paraded on Fox television? How many believed that it was really akin to the cold virus, even though it was infecting thousands and killing on average over 1,000 people per day? How many might have been alive today if they were told to take the disease seriously and take steps to protect themselves and their families from the deadly virus.

It is not enough to say that people bear personal responsibility for their own safety. While this is true, we cannot ignore the power of the mass media and its influence on the minds of those who get their information from it. Many are likely to believe what they hear, especially if they are steadfast supporters of particular anchors or news analysts on a network. That is the nature of the business.

The further question is what responsibility do a news media bear to its adherents? The canons of journalism demand fidelity to certain ethical standards. What happens when those standards are fragrantly breached? But an even more haunting question is that in light of a national emergency of the kind imposed by Covid-19, shouldn't there be some criminal liability for those who intentionally parade false narratives about the emergency which could result in harm to the public?

There is yet one other question to ask. What is the role of advertisers in all this? A network cannot survive without the strong support of advertisers. As is well known in the industry, advertisements/sponsorships are the mother's milk for the survival of any media house. As far as I know, publicly, there was no pulling of advertisements when these falsehoods were being paraded on Fox. There was no righteous indignation from corporate bodies that they would not support such falsehoods. So, in a real sense, by their own silence and quiescence, they aided, wittingly or unwittingly, these narratives and the possible deaths of thousands of Americans who once bought their products or used their services. The pictures of the chief executives of these companies should be pinned on a hall of shame. Obviously for them, profit superseded concern for humanity.

As the virus continues its deadly rampage through the country, the Trump administration has clearly given up on any desire to put up a robust fight against it. As he said, it is what it is. In the meantime, it is forecasted that millions more will become infected, with metrics indicating that over 400,000 will die if the present inaction persists to the end of the year. This does not have to happen. Thousands of lives can be saved by people simply wearing a mask, but the president has no visceral interest in this being done. He continues to hold indoor political rallies in which thousands gather and where many do not wear a mask. He does not wear one himself.

He simply does not seem to care if people get sick or die from this virus. Americans must ask themselves whether he is the kind of leader they would want to lead them after January 20, 2021, when we may be well under the greatest onslaught from the virus. I hope enough Americans will truly see the president for who he is in this hour of distress and engulfing darkness and say to him on November 3, "Mr. President, you're fired!"

# CHAPTER FOUR

## THE CASE AGAINST DONALD TRUMP-

## PART TWO- Racial Bigotry, Social Injustice and the Great Economic Divide

*We must strive to be moved by a generosity of spirit that will enable us to outgrow the hatred and conflicts of the past-* Nelson Mandela

To be sure, the matter of racial bigotry and injustice and the growing social and economic inequality that these have spawned in America, predate President Trump. What is happening today is that by his words and actions he has given life and currency to these things to an almost wearying level in the country.

The police killing of George Floyd in Minneapolis brought into sharp focus the systemic racism that has scarred the nation's conscience. Let us recall that on Memorial Day 2020, when the nation was remembering with gratitude thousands of their fellow men and women who had died in various wars down through the years, a young black man by the name of George Floyd was detained by the police in Minneapolis. He had tendered a $20 note which was deemed counterfeit by the store owner who promptly called the police. They arrived on the scene and decided to arrest him. He was placed on the ground after he had been handcuffed.

One of the officers, Derek Chauvin, placed his knee on Floyd's neck and kept it there for close to nine minutes, despite Floyd's plea that he could not breathe. Bystanders saw that he was clearly in distress and called on Chauvin to lift his restraint. He did not. Amazingly, three other officers who were on the scene with Chauvin did not deter his behavior.

The tragic outcome of this sad episode is that Floyd died. His death triggered protests and violent outbreaks across the country and in some parts of the world. Black people had had enough. Years of marginalization and of being treated as second class citizens in the land of their birth had now reached a tipping point. Furthermore, the Covid-19 pandemic had laid bare the glaring disparities and inequalities in the system by the extent to which it was decimating the black population when compared to the white. Too many blacks were exposed to the virus at their places of work. The virus laid bare the institutional and structural racism in the deployment of health resources to communities of color.

Floyd's death and the police brutality that spawned it, brought to the fore centuries of neglect of the black community. They were not prepared to have their voice silenced this time around. The day of reckoning had arrived. The tragic death of Floyd would be the torch that would light a new path to freedom for blacks. Chauvin's knee on his neck was reminiscent of the noose that ended the lives of many of their forebears. Floyd's cry, "I can't breathe," was the rallying cry to end black oppression and marginalization in America.

Black outrage against systemic racism in America is understandable. One can also understand when members of the white population, especially those who have done well, say that there is no systemic racism in the country. It is either that they don't understand what the term means or they are being disingenuous in their lack of appreciation of its meaning. Having benefitted substantially from the resources of an oppressive system, they are blinded to how marginalization of black and brown communities has become interwoven into the very fabric of the society and how this has contributed to their impoverishment since the days of slavery.

It was refreshing to see the hundreds if not thousands of white, especially young people, who marched with blacks in spontaneous outrage against the killing of Floyd. And this was not new because many white people before them marched with blacks in the heady days of the Civil Rights movement. As many chanted "black lives matter" it was clear that this was not just a cry to end police brutality, but a clarion call that signaled the end to the haunting specter of systemic racism that has bedeviled the society for too long. It was also a rejection of the America written of in the history books which blacks find it difficult to identify with.

For example, they cannot identify themselves in the "WE" mentioned by Thomas Jefferson in the preamble to the declaration of independence. Jefferson meant well and the document he penned is one of the most enduring documents in human history. But while it spoke to the relevance of the white community it cruelly excluded blacks and native Americans.

For Jefferson was himself an owner of slaves and thus subscribed to the philosophy that they were mere cattle to be used for white capitalist enterprise and prosperity.

Since their forebears were not recognized as human beings and codified as such, blacks know that what was mentioned in that founding document did not apply to them. Neither did it apply to the native Indian population that had been decimated or otherwise herded into reservations and their culture defaced and erased in so many ways. Interestingly, neither did it include women, even white women, who had no right to vote.

We must not forget that the Civil War in which more Americans died than in all wars the country has fought in combined, was fought because planters in the Southern States refused to end slavery. Even when they grudgingly accepted defeat, the southerners were not willing to integrate with the black population. Thus, began the era of Jim Crow and the degrading policy of segregation which defined it. It is the Jim Crow era which further hardened and cemented the institutional racism that is at vogue in the society. Sometimes it raises its ugly head in well-defined ways such as police brutality largely to black men. Other times, and mostly so, it is subtle and is seen in housing and health disparities, poor public amenities in black neighborhoods, disparities in educational opportunities for blacks further resulting in their economic marginalization, wage discrimination, the disproportionate incarceration of blacks vis-à-vis the white population, and a host of other maladies that exclude blacks from real participation in the country they call the United States of America.

The immediate results of Jim Crow's depredations are not readily known to the oppressive class, but to the oppressed. What is striking about the history of Jim Crow is how readily accepted were the icons of oppression such as statues and other public monuments that were erected to the memory of those who were dedicated to the dissolution of the United States. Public statues are erected to show admiration and even veneration, but in the case of Confederate officers and their enablers, they are icons of treasonous men. Not only were they prepared to split the country in two, but they wanted to maintain a system which has been the most loathsome attack on humanity.

It is also loathsome that although the South lost the Civil War, and although the writing of history belongs to the victors, Jim Crow ensured that the vanquished got to write the history of that era. And wrote it they did ensuring that institutions were put in place to keep blacks from the centers of political and economic power. So, when blacks march under the banner that black lives matter, it is not just a statement that these statues must be pulled down and history corrected, but that years of ignominy must give way to a new paradigm of respect and inclusion for the black community.

This is what the Trump administration does not understand when it supports white supremacists and defends the continuance of statues of traitors and seditionists such as General Lee. The president's stubbornness to see this glaring fact reveals where his heart truly is. It is certainly not in a good place as was clear when white supremacists and neo-Nazis marched in Charlottesville, Virginia, with burning torches against black protesters. Trump said there were "good" people on both sides, giving moral equivalency to righteous indignation against inequality and injustice and barefaced bigotry, hatred and racism. His open support for these groups and his embrace of Jim Crow history, is an insult to the nation's collective intelligence.

While black outrage against racial injustice is clear and understandable, it is not so clear or readily understood what is to be done about it. At the center of racism is fear. It is fear that gave rise to laws which institutionalized it so that it would become a protective barrier between the white ruling class and blacks. It is fear that continues to drive it today.

President Trump has proved himself a master at stoking the fear inherent in racism. It is seen in his overt and covert support of white supremacist groups, his defense of confederate icons, and in his present campaign to divide suburban neighborhoods by warning of a coming wave of invasion that will change the character of those neighborhoods. There is no doubt as to the color of the invaders that Trump has in mind. He has to scare women enough in these communities so that they can turn to him in November as the knight in shining armor to save them.

The bottom-line is that the president cannot be trusted to lead a conversation on racial healing in America. We are not just talking about the scars of racism, for racism remains an open wound on which Mr. Trump is attempting to pour salt. As Joe Biden pertinently said, he is pouring fuel on the fire of racism. He is a fruitful contributor to the racial bile that is flowing through the country. If by some bewitching brew he does retain power, do not expect in his lame duck years to be preoccupied with such grandiose abstractions as deep and abiding love and concern for black people. He will continue to be mercurial in his approach as he sends his federal agents to "dominate" towns and cities where blacks protest. He will bully them into submission to prove that he is the law and order president.

The challenge in the present outrage is how to harness all this righteous anger into well thought out policies to arrest the problem. This will not be easy for racism is a persistent and stubborn problem. It requires openness and empathetic leadership which can inspire in people the courage to face the problem with equal stubborn determination. The problem can no longer be ignored or treated with tokenism. It will not just disappear over time as some believe the coronavirus will. The time has come for radical change and this calls for strong, resolute leadership of the kind that Mr. Trump cannot provide. For this reason, it is time for all citizens of goodwill who believe in equity and justice to say to him: "you're fired."

## The Growing Economic Divide

From the start of his presidency, the president determined that if he were to win a second term this would rest heavily on the performance of the economy. He looked to the stock market as the chief measurement of the strength of the economy. If the market indices rose with some consistency in a given week, that was a sign to him of economic resilience.

Thus, the central theme of the Republican convention was the great job that Mr. Trump had done with the economy. The shambles that the economy is in with rising unemployment and the headwinds that companies faced, were largely ignored. Each speaker on the economy, such as his chief economic adviser, Larry Kudlow, lionized his handling of the economy and how unsafe it would be in the hands of Joe Biden.

The rosy picture that Republicans have of the economy bear no resemblance to the real state of the economy. It is true that the S&P 500 and the other stock indices have been showing great resilience, the S&P itself reaching its highest levels in August. Some of the biggest companies, largely in the tech sector such as Amazon, Google, Apple, Netflix and Tesla, to name a few, have showed astronomical gains. In one day, the heads of three of these companies made over $75 billion. Apple in August became the richest company in human history with a market capitalization of over two trillion dollars. This is more than the size of the GDP of over 50 countries combined.

But what is happening on the stock market or on Wall Street bears no relationship to what is happening in the real economy, on Main Street, where most of us reside. To emphasize, there is a gulf between the real economy and the financial markets. Despite Republican mantra of how great the economy is doing under Trump, the truth is that the economy today is more depressed than it has ever been since the Great

Depression. This is certainly the case since the financial crisis and the Great Recession of 2008.

It is true that the economy did grow and produce jobs during the three years under the Trump administration, but this has been slower and weaker than the three years under President Obama. Trump and the Republicans talk as if the Obama Administration never existed. Yet, the gains that the president boasts about are the results of the economic stabilization policies embarked on by the previous administration. Trump and the Republicans will never admit this because it goes against their narrative of a failed Obama presidency. For Trump personally it would be a violation of his own desire to obliterate anything that bears the former president's name.

Despite being handed a fairly robust economy, Trump failed to build on these gains and so the economy has been anemic at best. According to data from the US Bureau of Labor Statistics, there have been 1.5 million fewer jobs under Trump than there were under Obama. Trump stands seventh in line of the last 11 presidents when it comes to annualized gross domestic product (GDP) growth. According to data from the US Bureau of Economic Analysis, growth has actually slowed during the last three years under Trump.

To achieve this tepid growth, Mr. Trump and his Republican colleagues who controlled the Congress, resorted to the greatest tax heist in modern history under the 2017 Tax and Jobs Act. This largely favored big businesses and wealthy Americans while sending the deficit into the stratosphere.

There can perhaps be no greater indication of Republican hypocrisy than the about face turn the party has taken on deficit spending. This started under Reagan, became a central core of Bush (the Younger) economic policy, and has now reached its zenith under Trump.

The great tax giveaway represented the greatest transfer of wealth from the poor and the middle class to the wealthiest 10 percent of the population who neither needed nor deserved it. It was intended to fulfill Trump's promises to his wealthy donors. Former Goldman Sachs alum and Secretary of the Treasury, Steve Mnuchin, said the tax package would stimulate growth in the economy at a sustained rate of 3 percent of GDP. He believed that growth would be so spectacular that in time it would increase federal tax revenues by two trillion dollars. This would happen by a trickle-down effect that would permeate throughout the economy to the benefit of all.

I do not need to tell you that none of this happened. Since the tax heist the deficit has ballooned to over one trillion dollars, up from $681 billion in 2017. The inescapable truth is that before the tax cut, American industry was not short of capital. With the lowest interest rates in history, buoyed by the easy money pumped into the economy by the Federal Reserve under its Quantitative Easing (QE) program, the country was awash with loanable capital.

With all this money sloshing around in the economy businesses on Main Street found it difficult to get loans. Mega businesses which had easy access to capital failed to ramp up production as they should and largely used to money to buy back stocks, reward shareholders with dividends or otherwise investing it or perhaps even moving it to offshore accounts. Real production, especially in the manufacturing sector, languished. It was therefore no surprise that economic growth has remained anemic up to the time when the pandemic struck.

The pandemic was sudden and catastrophic for the economy. It was a shock to the body politic never before experienced since the Great Depression. By the end of March, millions of Americans were out of a job as businesses were shut down. Although there has been an uptick in employment hovering around 10 percent, unemployment has remained stubbornly worrying. Many who lost their jobs face the grim prospect of not getting them back.

Under the Coronavirus Aid, Relief, and Economic Security (CARES) Act, the federal government was able to bring relief and support to individuals and businesses throughout the country. There were provisions for unemployment insurance payments of $600, but these have all expired. At the time of writing, the President and the Congress have been unable to reach a consensus to bring further relief to beleaguered Americans who are finding it difficult to pay their bills and who face evictions from rented dwellings.

Even before the payments expired, many families were finding it difficult to feed their families. The food banks throughout the country are under stress as millions of Americans turn to them for help. One can expect greater hardships as the virus continues its deadly trek through the country. The misery index for a lot of people has gone up and there is every indication that this will be the case in the foreseeable future.

A recent survey indicated that close to 60 percent of Americans cannot readily find $400 in the event of an emergency. This was before the pandemic struck. This is a tragic indictment on the richest nation on earth and one which boasts more multi-billionaires than any other. Can you imagine what things are like for many people who do not have a paycheck? Yet, Trump and his minions are selling the false narrative of a strong economy. Jared Kushner, Chairman of the Universe in Trump's orbit, and a major spokesman for the administration, echoed his boss by trumpeting that the economy would be "rocking" by July. It is rocking alright, just like a boat caught in the maelstrom of a raging storm. But this president and his backers will say and do anything to support his delusional quest for a second term.

It is only the Republicans who will not admit that it is the administration's incompetent handling of the coronavirus crisis why the economy is in the parlous state that it is. In the first six months of 2020 it contracted by 10.6 percent, the fastest decline since the Great Depression. Needless to say, black Americans have been affected more negatively by the fallout in the closure of black-owned businesses (see the Federal Reserve Bank of New York report on black-owned business, August 4, 2020). Despite Trump's boast of what he has done for the economic advancement of blacks, the median household income for black families continues to decline when compared to whites. As the virus continues to hobble the economy expect more layoffs and furloughs which will disproportionately affect black families.

The continuing sad truth is that while the economy continues to do well for the top 10 percent, who can own stocks and other investment products, the ordinary American does not, and in many instances cannot, get any income from capital gains. The decks are stacked against them even though they may be working at two or more jobs.

When the economy is this skewed against the interests of the average American there is less disposable income to drive demand in the economy. And demand is what we need to build in a high consumer society as America is. The present danger is that more than ever before too many businesses lack consumers who are willing and able to buy their products and services.

To press the point further, if people cannot earn a livable wage their propensity to consume is severely cauterized. This is especially so when you add other extraneous stress factors to their already overburdened pockets such as taking away their health care as Mr. Trump seems so desperate to do. Business people who are in the real world are acutely aware of the declining ability of Americans to consume. They see the wage stagnation and how many Americans have to be struggling to survive. They will have to recalibrate their businesses so as not to go bankrupt.

Many have already gone this route. According to the American Bankruptcy Institute (ww.abi.org) more retailers have gone bankrupt in the first eight months of 2020 than in all of 2008, the year of the great financial meltdown. Across all industries, Chapter 11 filings surged 52 percent in July over the same period in 2019. And we seem to be just getting started. As the economy contracts further, expect many more bankruptcies to occur. Many smaller businesses in the retail and restaurant industries will simply disappear never to return. As long as the virus continues at its peak point of residency in our lives there will not be any rocking recovery as the president and his fellow dreamers would wish. Remember the proposition I made earlier: there can be no robust opening of the economy without a robust containment of the virus. It is that simple, though hard to do.

Under Mr. Trump, the economic inequalities in the country are bound to widen. Too many people see the rich getting richer while the poor have to settle for the crumbs that fall from the table of their masters. If you push for economic equality you are labelled a socialist. Social justice is no longer a language of biblical prophetic outrage, but an essential element of socialist thinking for many in the evangelical world. And this is unfortunate, for this thinking rejects one of the bedrock principles of the gospel message which is to seek social and economic justice for the poor and oppressed. God still has an option for the oppressed.

Trump has clearly staked his political future on the side of Dives, the rich man in Jesus parable of Dives and Lazarus mentioned in Luke 16: 19-31. His heart is clearly not with the Lazaruses of this world who are forced to eat the crumbs that fall from the tables of the rich. He neither has the inclination, the disposition or sense of empathy that are needed to lessen the gulf between those who have and those who don't. He seems committed more than ever to widen the gulf between the two. If he gets the chance, he will not hesitate to get another tax heist for his rich friends even if this deepens the gulf between the rich and the poor in this country. Therefore, the fundamental inequality in our economic arrangement is not something that I believe he is even capable of addressing. It is time for the marginalized; the person who is living from paycheck to paycheck and yet have to be working harder than ever; the young person who daily sees the prospects of a better life vanishing before him or her, to say to him, "Mr. President, you're fired!"

# CHAPTER FIVE

## THE CASE AGAINST DONALD TRUMP

### PART THREE- The Loss of American Respectability Around the World

*The danger for the world is not an America that is too eager to immerse itself in the affairs of other countries, but that it may disengage, creating a vacuum of leadership that no other nation is willing to fill* -Barak Obama

As I write, the borders of the European Union, Canada and a few other countries are closed to Americans. This is a result of America's inability to control the spread of the coronavirus in its own borders, and the understandable threat of infection that this represents for those countries.

Again, this did not have to happen, but as we know America is the only leading industrial country that has failed to bring the virus under control. The world cannot understand why the richest country in the world blessed with the most brilliant scientists, institutions of learning, powerful transnational corporations and having the most powerful military, could have buckled so badly to the virus. Angela Merkel, Chancellor of Germany and the de facto leader of the European Union, if not the free world, put it best:

*We are seeing at the moment that the pandemic can't be fought with lies and disinformation, and neither can it be with hatred and agitation.*

This is an obvious reference to leaders like Trump, who, as we noted above, has conducted a campaign of disinformation and outright deception about the existential threat the virus poses to the American people.

As things stand today, America is a pariah in the world. It has been said that there was a time when the world feared America, but now it pities it. But if Trump gets a second term, the world may yet fear it again. He signaled in his first campaign for the presidency what his intentions were. His vision was "America First," which was part of his overall plan to make America great again. The net result of this policy was the shrinking of America's influence in the world as the president embarked on a number of initiatives which left no one in doubt that a new sheriff was in town and things were going to be radically different.

One of the first initiatives was the issuing of an Executive Order banning citizens from designated Muslim countries from entering the country for a defined period. Then there was the obsession with building a wall on the Southern border with Mexico, a campaign pledge that he felt committed to fulfill and for which Mexico would pay. As we know, Mexico hasn't paid a cent. The real intention behind Trumps obsession is to severely restrict Latin American immigration into America. I have already commented on the humanitarian disaster that this policy became with the separation of children from their parents and the inhumane conditions in which many, even today, are being held.

It became apparent that if Trump unilaterally had the power to wall off America from the rest of the world, he would do so. There is a thinly veiled racism that attends his obsession in this matter. He has shown a clear disdain for black and brown people from countries he has designated "s...hole" countries while acknowledging a clear preference for immigrants from countries like Norway. National leaders who demonstrate a "walled off" mentality are clearly not accommodative of people who are different from them.

## The Russian Connection

At every turn, Mr. Trump's behavior on the world stage seems destined to make America a pariah state. He has succeeded in alienating many of America's traditional allies by his impolitic behavior at international conferences and his irascible signal that America can go it alone. The big elephant sitting in the room is always Russia and its mercurial leader, Vladimir Putin. Before he won office, America's chief international partners were puzzled at Trump's accommodative posture on the Russian dictator. Somehow, they may have put this down to a lack of intelligence on Putin, and hoped, as many Americans did, that he would at least follow the line that his predecessors had done as he gained experience on the job.

But, alas, this was not to be. To the chagrin and amazement of America's key allies, Trump doubled down on his open support of the Russian president to the point of discrediting his own intelligence agencies' negative reporting on Putin's action. The most galling has been his repeated questioning of the CIA, NSA, and FBI assessment of Russia's interference in the 2016 presidential election. At the Asian-pacific Economic Cooperation summit Trump asserted that Putin told him that he did not meddle in the elections, and he believed him. This was either the highest form of presidential naivete or the admission of one who is beholden to and holds a hidden debt to the Russian autocrat.

From reports from the FBI, there are clear signs that Russia is meddling in this year's election as well. Trump, in an interview with ABC's anchor, George Stephanopoulos, without smiling, admitted that he would accept any help that comes to him from a foreign source. There should be no doubt that he would hesitate accepting such help from Russia. His silence on Russian malfeasance must be a matter of grave concern for America. His intelligence agencies raised alarm in a recent report that Putin has placed a bounty on American troops in Afghanistan. There was even indication that payment has already been paid for such action.

Again, Trump has denied receiving such a report. Even if he did not get a report, I will take the intelligence agencies' word any day over Trump's. At any rate, the mere mention that there is such a report should have aroused some outrage in him to even look into it. He should have been moved to even utter a statement that if this is so he would take resolute measures to protect the troops and punish those who would wish to harm them. But there was nothing. Nada.

America's allies in Europe have been very perplexed at how easily Trump is accommodating Putin's wishes in the dismemberment of the North Atlantic Treaty Organization (NATO). There is no doubt that Putin would be the happiest man on earth if NATO should disappear overnight. Trump has lambasted his allies for the non-payment of their financial obligations to the organization. He recently withdrew 12,000 troops from Germany in defiance of NATO's wishes, but chiefly to poke a finger in the eyes of the German leader Merkel with whom he has had a prickly relationship. It no doubt pleased Putin as this signaled a further weakening of the alliance that he has left no doubt he hates.

The break up of the USSR was one of the saddest events for Putin. His lifetime ambition in politics is to restore the glory days when the Iron Curtain as Churchill described it, wrapped its tentacles across a wide swath of Europe. It would be naïve to assume that such ambitions have died. I would predict that if Trump wins a second term, Putin will be emboldened to advance his ambitions. His annexation of the Crimea was the first shot to the world that he means business. This is just a template for what is to come if his apparent ally in the White House retains power. This would exacerbate hostilities and instability in the world perhaps to a level we have never witnessed before.

## The Chinese Connection/Challenge

China may yet represent a greater challenge to America than Russia does. It's formidable economy, growing military power and its influence in the world, place it far ahead of Russia as a real bother to America. It is a challenge and an opportunity depending on how relations with China is handled.

There is no doubt that China has made tremendous strides over the last 20 years. As a net debtor to the Chinese, there are those who believe that China will surpass America as the leading economic power, perhaps in the next 20 years. I believe that this is an exaggerated view, but the challenge is formidable.

For good or ill, the challenge has become more intense under Trump's presidency. In his campaign for the office, he was quite emphatic that trading relationships with the Chinese government would change radically. He believed that the Chinese were ripping off America both in the lopsided trading arrangements and China's theft of American intellectual property.

This is one area in which I find some agreement with Trump. Before Trump, it is estimated that China exported to America more than three times the goods and services that America did. This was neither free trade nor fair trade, for while America was open in its trading arrangements with that country, the Chinese were very restrictive, making it difficult for American goods and services to flow easily into that country. The fact that China was a signatory to the World Trade Organization (WTO) made little difference, for China has been known not to play by the rules or to be too bothered by their enforcement.

China simply wanted to eat its cake and take it home at the same time and America over the years has allowed them to have a feast. The net result is that China has built up a massive surplus estimated in the region of about three trillion dollars largely on its trade imbalance with the rest of the world, America being the chief cornerstone of this imbalance.

The Chinese might be more surprised than any American that they have been allowed to get away with this for so long. Succeeding presidential candidates pledged on campaign trails to deal with the "China problem" but as soon as they got into office such promises were forgotten. This has been the case ever since Nixon's rapprochement with China and the granting of Most Favored Nation status to that country. This was essentially a policy of appeasement of the Chinese which gave them privileged access to the US marketplace despite its abysmal record on human rights.

When Trump came into office all of this changed. From very early in his administration he signaled to the Chinese that things would change; that it would no longer be business as usual. He was right to reexamine America's overall trading arrangements with China and to come down heavily on the theft of American intellectual property by that country.

But in typical mercurial style he has approached the problem with a sledgehammer instead of with the chiseled reasoning that you need to have in dealing with the proud Chinese. He imposed draconian tariff barriers on the country reminiscent of the era of protectionism. As night follows day, China hit back with draconian measures of its own. The figures are still being calculated, but what is emerging is that American farmers, especially in the Midwest, have been severely and negatively impacted by these measures. Trump has had to provide subsidies to these farmers, as many family farms faced bankruptcy and even now are finding it hard to cope.

Trump claims that the country is reaping a tremendous benefit from his tough China policy. How much of this is true is left to be seen. What we do know is that the American consumer is facing the brunt of these draconian measures. Tariffs are an indirect tax on consumers' pockets and we have seen inflation in the price of goods imported from China.

While I do not agree with how Trump has approached the revision of the country's trading relationship with China, I still believe that China stands to lose more in a trade war with the US than the US does with them. Although China has four times the population of America, the country is heavily dependent on the US marketplace for sale of its goods and services. Despite its large population, the Chinese marketplace is not robust and sophisticated enough to absorb China's output of goods and services. It will increasingly depend on the world market, especially the US market to do so. That they are capable of this output is already evident. The Chinese have a legendary work ethic which will stand them well into the future. It is this work ethic that has resulted in the considerable expansion of the Chinese middle class which means that more people are being lifted out of poverty.

There is another aspect of the "Chinese problem" that may be more problematic than that of trade. This is the rising influence of China on the world stage. The extension of its influence throughout the world is significant at a time when America's is shrinking. This is a direct result of the political polarization in Washington and the resultant divisions in the country, which have been made worse under Trump.

Furthermore, Mr. Trump's unilateral dealings with China, fueled by his go-it-alone posture, has prevented him from working with his global partners in curbing China's growing influence. Indeed, the hostile posture that he has maintained with America's chief allies has been a boon to Chinese hegemony in the world. For while the West is distracted, China has moved in to fill the void and to present itself as a global benefactor worthy of consideration.

While American politicians demonize and make political cannibals of each other, China has quietly, smartly, deftly and strategically been winning friends and influencing people around the world. They are actively investing in Africa, Latin America and the Caribbean region. Sitting on close to over three trillion United States dollars of reserves, they have the economic muscle to do this. It is true that the country has suffered a setback due to the economic fallout from the coronavirus, but there are signs that it is beginning to bounce back. The sad truth is that America cannot embark on this kind of aggressive global investment anytime soon as it would be doing so on borrowed money and rising deficits, not on real income. The Chinese are doing so on real income and they are doing so smartly.

In Latin America and the Caribbean region, literally in America's backyard, the Chinese have stepped up their investments in infrastructure projects, largely in road building and repair and in the oil and gas industry. The pace of Chinese investment in Africa has been even more frenetic. Through their Ex-Im Bank credit facilities, loans to African countries have increased without the strictures that often accompany World Bank or International Monetary Fund requirements.

Chinese investment is conducted on a pragmatic basis with a clear understanding of non-interference in the domestic affairs of the countries in which they invest. Countries that receive their assistance are not too constrained by issues of Chinese violation of human rights, but by the capital they receive to develop their economies. This is not to say they are not concerned about human rights violation, but that they consider their countries economic growth to be paramount in their relationship with China.

It would be naïve to assume that Chinese global investment is built largely on their benevolence, philanthropy or goodwill. It is certainly predicated on their geopolitical strategic interests. In the Caribbean, for example, a great deal of its involvement is tied to its "one China" policy which is intended to lure these island states away from Taiwan. It is being seen that Taiwan cannot match Chinese financial mettle in this area. The Chinese will not admit it readily, but it is clear that their objective is to counter American influence in the world and to emerge as a superpower that can challenge the supremacy of America globally. Except for their military posture in the South China Sea region, China's reach in the world is not by flexing its military muscle, but by a stealthy "economic diplomacy" which seems to be working.

How America counters this growing influence is left to be seen, but what seems clear to me is that Mr. Trump's bullying tactics will not work. Neither will geopolitical hysteria nor knee-jerk reactions which create unnecessary tension between the two countries. China will not allow itself to be bullied nor punished for perceived human rights abuses by the United States when, under Trump, it can make some equivalency between what it does and the obvious human rights abuses against blacks in America.

Flexing military muscles is a non-starter given China's status as a nuclear power. Having been emboldened by its economic success, China will not bow to the demand of any world power for what it would term as meddling in its internal affairs. Sanctions, grand standing and big talk will not work. Washington's best bet is to work within the framework of economic openness and to nudge the Chinese to the inevitable social change which the expanding middle class will demand. This, incidentally, should have been its approach to the Cuban problem. For China, this will demand more trade and cultural exchanges, not less. But trade has to be conducted on a basis that is both fair and free. The Chinese must recognize that equitable trading arrangements are what the world demands today. There can be no compromise on this and the Chinese know it.

Despite all the hostile rhetoric directed to the Chinese by the Trump administration, and China replying in tone, China has no interest in a weak or weakened America. The bald truth is that an economically weakened America does not increase the prospects of a prosperous China. If China can get away with the current imbalance in trade with both countries it will happily do so. They may not say so loudly but no country is more conscious than China that they need a strong America in order to remain competitive and strong themselves. This is why they will not refuse to finance US debt anytime soon. Why rock the boat when they can benefit royally from the arrangement? If they have to respond to real or perceived threats they will, but they are not frightened by the often loudmouthed and frothy bullying tactics employed by Trump.

America must continue to prod China towards being a more open society that embraces full freedom for its people and which upholds their right to self-determination. This is a critical American value which is non-negotiable. It is by being faithful to its own homespun values that America can counter the Chinese influence in the world. It is pellucidly clear to me that a larger percentage of the world will embrace America's values for an open and free society than they will China's close and often oppressive denial of those values.

People are not risking their lives and that of their families to live in China but they are doing so to get to America. America must remain that beacon on the hill that all freedom loving people in the world can believe in. In the next 10 years America's relationship with China will be the most definitive factor in world diplomacy. It will not be Russia, which does not have the economic muscle of China, and whose weak, corrupt and shriveled political and economic structure leaves so much to be desired.

Americans must ask who is best able to lead America in the next four years of that ten. The one who uses belligerence and threats to get conformity or the one who employs reasoned dialogue and hard diplomacy when needed, to effect change? The one who can understand the philosophical framework of particular polices and their implications for a stable global environment, or the one whose incuriosity and intemperance, fueled by delusional thinking about his own abilities, can only widen tensions and perhaps cause military confrontation? The next election will answer these questions. I have no doubt as to what the answers should be.

## Trump's Clear Preference for Autocratic Values

One of the bedrock values that has made America respectable in the world is its steadfast defense of human rights and the aspirations of all people to be free. This is what has fanned American patriotic values since the founding of the nation. It is what lies at the very root of protests against racial injustice. In the last three years of the Trump presidency, these values have been placed under great strain in America. One of the unprecedented characteristics of his presidency is the extent to which he has harbored autocratic notions of the wide powers that he has as president.

In the early days of the pandemic, he believed that his executive powers allowed him to tell the governors what to do or to even override decisions they may make. He has been aided in this thinking by people such as his attorney general who clearly believes in the inordinate powers that have been granted to the executive branch of government. He has been further aided by fawning sycophants in the evangelical community who have paraded the almost messianic notion that Trump is a man sent by God to heal the nation's wounds, a belief he may harbor in his abilities to get things done.

Perhaps the most worrying aspect of his autocratic longings can be seen in how he has addressed largely black protesters on the streets of America. The president knows that between now and November 3, he cannot rely on the economic argument to win. So, true to his disposition to distract attention from his own failings, he has resorted to fear as a political tactic. It is fear that white suburban neighborhoods will be devalued by "savage hordes" (my words) that may invade them; fear of violence by black anarchist groups rioting in the streets and fear of a socialist takeover of America that will crash the economy.

This fearmongering is the only tool that Trump has left in his political bag of tricks, but it will not work as Americans have seen the folly of it. It is no surprise that he has targeted Democratic run cities and municipalities in spreading his message of fear. Militia groups loyal to Trump have been known to stoke violence in these areas. Members of this group can be seen walking around with rifles and demonstrators have been killed. The president has not condemned these obvious acts of provocation and intimidation. They obviously give him the excuse he needs to send paramilitary personnel into these areas to quell disturbances and to reinforce the narrative in the minds of his supporters that he is the law and order president. This tactic is one that is clear out of the fascist's playbook and is not unlike those employed by fascists of a bygone era in twentieth century Italy and Germany and in today's Russia.

Trump's autocratic impulses represent a grave danger for this country. He has shown admiration for dictators and strongmen around the world. His fawning admiration or perhaps fear of Russian president Vladimir Putin has now been well established. He speaks glowingly of his relationship with Kim Jong Un, the North Korean dictator, who was a pariah in the world until Trump started to give him some respectability. Trump believes that because he can have a good relationship with these leaders that he is loved by them. But they have read him and understand his profile as a leader who craves attention. Putin especially understands this. He knows that Trump is superficial and can be easily played to do his bidding.

He is obviously impressed by the military parades that he has seen in places like North Korea, China, Russia and France. On a trip to France in July 2017, the president observed the Bastille Day military parade. He described it as one of the most beautiful parades he has ever seen and immediately dreamt of having his own July 4 Independence Day parade, with the deployment of tanks and fighter jets flyovers. This shocked many in the country especially in the military. It was a violation of the long-held convention that America does not parade its military might as this is contrary to every democratic instinct that the country possesses. Most importantly, it revealed a man yearning to have his ego stoked by having the world getting a glimpse at the vast military power over which he presides.

In soaring rhetoric, Mr. Trump sometimes speak of the values of freedom that has made America great, but at times he betrays that he does not have a visceral feel for those values. The world looks on in consternation at what America is becoming; how its institutions are being undermined by a president who demonstrates a clear disposition to autocratic rule; how a proud nation that was forged out of the anvil of immigration is being shriveled and walled off from the rest of the world. It is disgusted at an America that petulantly withdraws from treaties and organizations which are intended to make the world safer and healthier, such as the Iran nuclear deal, the Paris climate accord, and the World Health Organization-in the midst of a pandemic. The country's legendary generosity has been replaced by a parochial notion of America first. America is increasingly being viewed as a country that its leading allies cannot count on in times of a real global emergency.

November 3 will be a critical turning point in America's relationship with the world. If the president is re-elected, I believe it will be an America that will continue to be a real embarrassment to the world. Then, all bets would be off as there will be a loud global sigh of frustration. America will be seen as an undependable partner and so will become more isolated as its leading allies realign themselves to go into new directions without America's help. So, on November 3, I believe the world, at least its leading allies, are giving Americans one last chance to get it right. I believe they are holding their collective breaths as to whether American voters will have the courage to say to this president, "Mr. President, you're fired!"

# CHAPTER SIX

## NOVEMBER 3, 2020- A DAY OF RECKONING FOR AMERICA

### Is This What Americans Really Want for the Next Four Years?

*When we are born, we cry that we are come to this great stage of fools*-William Shakespeare

In the preceding chapters I have briefly sought to set out the case against Trump's re-election as best as I know how and bearing true fidelity to the facts as I understand them. It is certainly not a complete assessment and a great deal more could be said. Like most Americans, I do not know Mr. Trump personally and so one has sought to rely on the facts concerning him both in terms of his own public utterances and actions in office and the many cogent analyses, based on fact, that have been presented by commentators and writers in the public sphere.

What I have gleaned from watching the president over the almost four years he's been in office is that he is not really a difficult person to read. I once heard his chief sidekick, Jared Kushner, say that the president is very transparent, and this is really true but not for the reasons Kushner might have intended. For while the president is like an open sieve, and thus can be easily read, he can also be quite closed and obscurantist when it comes to things he would want to keep hidden. We have seen this in his steadfast refusal to disclose his taxes and his ability to hide information from the Congress.

Nevertheless, the president is really what you see. He has one fatal flaw: predictability. This is based largely on his transactional approach to how he conducts his personal and business lives. It is how he has conducted his presidency. Praise him, say good things about him and he is your friend. Criticize him or say anything negative and you've earned an enemy, perhaps for life. Trump Has admitted that he does not run and hide when people "attack" him. When this happens, he will hit back hard as has been evident in his post-impeachment conduct.

Another element of his predictability is his enmity with the truth. Americans and diligent Trump watchers around the world have been aghast at how easily the president will lie to get himself out of a sticky situation or to embellish situations to make himself look good. This is dangerous for any country, especially one that is dependent upon the free flow of robust information that must be used to inspire policy and governance in general. If truth is what one makes it out to be and if it is all relative to one's idiosyncrasies or impulses, then facts be damned and the biggest liar gets to rule the day. From very early the stage was set for this project of misinformation when senior adviser to the president, Kellyanne Conway trumpeted to reporters what she called "alternative facts." Since then the Trump administration has lived in an alternate universe, and the country has been taken on a rollercoaster ride.

Another danger attending Trump's predictability is the extent to which he can be exploited by America's enemies. The uncanny former KGB operative, Vladimir Putin, understands Trump's nature and character quite well. He praised the president's intelligence and that was enough to get Trump on his side, quite apart from any other sword that might be hanging over the president's head in Russia. He can wring concessions out of him or at least get him to openly disavow things-such as his acceptance of Putin's word that he did not interfere in our elections. No other administration since the days of the Cold War or even before, has given Russia the solace it has enjoyed under President Trump. Can you imagine the Kremlin's elation when Trump shoved aside the findings of his intelligence agencies and embraced the word of their president instead?

Kim Jong Un, the North Korean dictator, understands this playbook quite well. He has exploited the president's naivete and need for praise. I had no doubt that Trump's forays into North Korea would bear no meaningful fruit. It was a grand soap opera that fizzled. North Korea got more out of the engagement than America did as Kim was made to look good on the world stage as one standing shoulder to shoulder with an American president. We are now at a most dangerous level with our relations with that country. Talks have stalled and there is no certainty as to how fast Kim is proceeding with his nuclear program.

Trump's relationship with Xi Jinping, consummate ruler of China, is less predictable. The Chinese are a complex people who cannot be easily read, and Xi is a master at this puzzle. What he and other world leaders who are chummy with president Trump know, is that he is notoriously incurious. By his own admission the president does not read much. After all, a man who is a very stable genius does not have to explore the world around him. It is safe to assume that he does not have an expansive vocabulary on many subjects as he ought. Being relatively inexperienced in world affairs and the art of diplomacy, Trump is like putty in the hands of people like Putin, Xi Jinping and Angela Merkel. They have to marvel at times that America could not have done better than unleashing such an uninformed person in their midst. Someone they cannot rely on for any philosophical depth or profound analysis of a particular subject. They must be bewildered at what he has to bring to a discussion and how different this is to their engagement with President Obama.

Is this why the president often appears so awkward in the few public meetings we see of him with these world leaders? He feels more comfortable in the presence of Putin and will go off to side chats with him whenever they meet. Putin will indulge his idiosyncrasies for a later benefit. Is this why Trump wants him to return as a member of the G7 group despite the strong and compelling reasons for his exclusion-invasion of the Ukraine, among other things?

The bottom-line is that the strongmen with whom Mr. Trump will want to be pals of do not have any deep respect for him-not his intellect, his lack of diplomacy or the egotistic persona that he brings to his relationship with them. They will exploit his naivete when they can, but they are very careful not to give anything up to him. The greatest beneficiary of Mr. Trump's naivete on the world stage has been Putin, but even he, being the uncanny person, has been very careful not to overplay his hand. He is no doubt wary that Trump may lose the election and he would have hell to pay when Joe Biden occupies the White House. If Trump wins then he will be laughing all the way to the bank. Should there be any doubt therefore, that he is actively working to ensure that Trump gets his second term?

**A Trump Second Term will be a Real Tragedy for America**
It has been said that November 3, 2020 will be an inflection point for America if President Trump should be re-elected to office. I am not a clairvoyant but I would like to put on my prophetic hat for a moment and present eight likely scenarios of what we could be faced with if this should happen. I would remind that prophetic criticism in the Old Testament was not so much foretelling events that would occur in the future, as it was forthtelling, based on the interpretation of events as they unfold in the present and their likely impact on the future. It is within this mindset that I venture these likely scenarios.

I do so within the context of Mr. Trump being 74 years of age. I believe in Maya Angelou's maxim that he must be taken for what he is. For almost four years as president he has shown us clearly how he thinks and what he is about. I believe that it is naïve to assume that at his age he can be expected to change fundamentally what he believes in.

Many, including journalists who bring him into our faces daily, are often aghast at some of the most outrageous statements or behavior of the president, as if to expect him to behave differently. I can under their reaction for I know that they have never seen a president behave like this in their lifetime. Also, their deference for the office of the presidency makes it hard to accept that a sitting president can so easily trash the norms and conventions that have made that office respectable. Because of my respect for the office of the presidency, to this day I find it difficult to call the president a liar, although I know he merits it. Somehow the term rings disrespectful of the office of the presidency, although not for the holder of the office at any given time. But that is just me and I know there are many who will hold an opposite view.

At his age and level of self-absorption, I do not expect to see Trump making any seismic change in his behavior or who he is as a person. I have often characterized him as an old oak tree that is incapable of being bent. He is who he is and short of divine intervention he will remain what he is for the years he has remaining on this earth. So, if he should get a second term one can only expect more of the same, if not worse as I will argue shortly. And this is simply not a case of Donald being Donald; it is the essence of who he is.

What is of greater concern to me is what he can do to this country which could turn anyone's weeping to open bawling and lament. For even if he loses, we could still be in serious peril. Let us understand that Trump remains president until January 20, 2021. Between November 3, 2020 and then, he will be a real lame duck, but given his proclivities and impulsivities, a dangerous lame duck. He will pose a graver danger if he refuses to leave office as many fear. Then, we would be faced with a constitutional crisis the likes of which we would not have seen since the Civil War. Having nothing to lose, expect some of the most egregious, unprecedented assaults on the integrity of the presidency. The area that will be most spectacularly abused is the pardon power of the president. In fact, Mr. Trump could be the most consequential lame duck that has served as president between the loss of an election and inauguration day.

But if he should win, I do not expect any spectacular change for the better. True to his transactional disposition, he will only adjust to meet desired ends and this is after he would have come under strong public pressure to change a policy. But he will change, not because he is convinced of the morality or saneness of a particular policy, but what benefits he can derive from changing course. He will continue to be a man with loose lips and as they say, loose lips sink ships. So far, the president has sunken a lot of "ships" by his patent falsehoods for which he expresses no regret, and which he often doubles down on.

## America Under a Trump Second Term

So, here are some likely scenarios of an America under a Trump second term.

1.**Further chaotic governance and a drifting, divided leadership of the country.** If Republicans control the White House and even one section of the Congress, we can expect four years of drifting, divided leadership, worse than what obtained in Trump's first term. The country would experience what I have termed "chaos on steroids" as the president's worse narcissistic impulses come to the fore. This will continue to be the most glaring aspect of a Trump second term.

Having overcome the findings of the Mueller report, escaped being removed from office after being impeached in the House of Representatives, and being rewarded for the most shambolic governance that this country has seen in a long time, he would see his re-election as a vindication of the "good" work he has been doing. If the election was a referendum on his time in office, which it truly would have been, then going into a second term, Trump would be right in seeing his victory as an endorsement of his performance, notwithstanding the tragedy that the first term would have visited upon the country. He will feel emboldened to push the boundaries of the presidency to limits that not even he would have imagined possible. He would be the king of all that he surveyed, a monarch par excellence, requiring almost divine admiration from his subjects. This is what his narcissistic impulses would tell him.

He would be beholden to no one and will make appointments to key offices in government which will further shock a nation, many still stupefied from thinking of four more years under him. Having been rewarded for being impeached and for his almost criminal handling of the Covid-19 pandemic, he would consider himself virtually unstoppable. I expect that his relationship with the Congress will be further strained. This is especially so if the Democrats should continue to control the

House of Representatives, or better, the entire Congress. If they hold the entire Congress, they will be able to enact legislation, and depending on their majority, to override any veto by the president. They may even be in a better position to impeach and remove the president from office. They would certainly be able to change the filibuster rule in the Senate, thus giving them greater leverage in passing legislation. If we have a divided Congress, the tension between Capitol Hill and the White House will be intensified and the country would have returned to business as usual.

The possibility of a divided Congress under a Trump second term should scare the bejesus out of any concerned American. We will have more of what we are experiencing now with a greater possibility for worse. Nothing will get done and the business of the nation may well be driven to a grinding halt. The only saving grace is to have a Congress controlled by the Democrats especially with an impressive majority in the Senate. This would be the greatest brake on the president's most powerful desires for autocratic rule.

Another likely effect of a drifting government under Trump is lethargy and apathy on the part of the president. The president will come alive to policies that he believes in, such as another tax heist for the rich, but generally, he will not have the energy or stamina for the work. After all, he will not be running for a third term, unless by some devilish intent he may want to move for an amendment to the constitution to allow him to run for still another term. This is not as farfetched as it may sound. Trump could see this move as a tool of distraction from doing the weightier requirements of his office. It would also be in line with what his apparent mentor in Russia did recently to cement himself in power.

But as old age creeps on, he will try to do more golfing, and is likely to become more aloof and reclusive in office. He is putting out the best he can now to get the second term, but once in he is likely to have no real stomach for the job. He is likely to get excited about projects that he feels deeply about such as a new tax cut for the rich, but I doubt that he would have the presence of mind or the stamina to grapple with serious issues which affect the daily life of ordinary Americans.

What would he have to lose? I suspect that he will double down on his trips to his exotic properties. But you will protest that Biden will be older than him. Fair. But Biden would seek to be more energetic as this would be his first term and there is so much to be done to restore and heal the nation. We have seen him as a hardworking vice-president and this would hardly change now that he would have the future of the country to consider in a first term.

The only saving grace that I see in all this is that if Trump wins the White House and the Democrats the Congress, the Democrats will be able to force his hand in legislating. He may want to get some things done, and he would prefer to work with what he has rather than put up a fight he will not win. At that stage, he would be willing to sign any legislation that comes to his desk, rather than put up a fight and having his veto overruled. He'd rather sit and watch Fox News than get into a real fight with the Democrats.

What is certain is that the partisan divide in Washington with its attending vitriol and even hatred will become more pronounced. The people are tired of this. We need somebody in the White House who is willing to work across the political aisle and seek to heal rather than further divide the nation. I believe that Joe Biden with his long experience in Congress and his work as Vice-President is best placed to do this.

2. **Greater militancy and hostility from white supremacist groups.** In its 2019 report, the Southern Poverty Law Center (SPLC) which tracks these groups, indicated that white nationalist hate groups increased 55 percent throughout the Trump era. This is indicative of a surging racist movement driven largely by fear of the changing demographic where whites would no longer be the dominant group in the society. It is no doubt driven also by Trumpian hate rhetoric and the tacit support that Trump seems to offer these groups.

There was a growth of 155 such groups in 2019 and this did not include groups such as the Ku Klux Klan, racist skinheads, Christian Identity and neo-Confederate groups. Overall, in 2019 there were 940 active hate groups, all expressing versions of white supremacist beliefs and advocating mass violence, terrorism and murder as part of their modus operandi.

There is absolutely no doubt in my mind that if Trump wins a second term, there will be further exponential growth in white supremacist groups. Only this time they will become more hostile and militant. Indeed, these too will become more emboldened. They will believe that their putative leader having triumphed is a vindication of their own cause and their undiluted support for him. Trump would no doubt have seen them as an indispensable element in his re-election to office and would want to reward them. He will be constrained not to be too open or overt in that support, but he will be more brazen in giving them succor.

Thus, hate speech will intensify which may issue into violence. Blacks will not take white violence against this sitting down, and so confrontations in the streets may become more pronounced. The "law and order" president will be moved to apply greater autocratic control of the streets. This time he will not be that benign.


3. **Greater debasement of the institutions of government**. Trump's sense of self already tells him that he can do almost anything and get away with it. He has been aided and abetted in this thinking by fawning acolytes in his party who are afraid of Trump's shadow falling on them. What would he have to lose if he wants to rachet up these impulses to have total control over the American government? Impeachment? This would only happen if the Democrats have a comfortable majority in both branches of Congress. If Trump returns to power, the thing that he will fear most is a Democratic control of Congress. But his stain will be seen in every department of government especially in the Secretariat of the Interior and the Environmental Protection Agency (EPA).

The institution that will be under the greatest peril is the department of justice. One would expect that if the president gets re-elected, William Barr will continue to be his attorney general. Many have already concluded, with good reason, that the attorney general has conducted himself in office as the president's attorney and not as the impartial chief law enforcer that the country should have. If Trump wins expect greater collusion and more egregious behavior from the two. Both men seem not to be constrained by any ethical dilemma that may arise in the conduct of their respective offices. A case in point is the desire to use taxpayers' resources to pay for the president's expenses in a defamation suit in an alleged rape case. *CNBC,* the business news outfit, reported that the Department of Justice would seek to join the suit on behalf of the president. If the litigant prevails, American taxpayers, and not the president, would be responsible for any monetary damages. (*CNBC Report, on September 9, 2020, Dan Mangan- White House asked DOJ to intervene in Trump rape defamation suit by E. Jean Carroll, taxpayers will pay damages if agency loses, Barr says*). Even if this is legal, it smells to high heavens from an ethical standpoint. In saner times, no attorney general would see it fit to use taxpayers' resources in this way. And no president with a modicum of decency would allow his or her name to be attached to something like this.

If he gets re-elected Trump's relationship with Barr will become more problematic. The attorney general would be emboldened to push his philosophy of the supreme executive to boundaries not seen before. This would further erode public trust in the institution, and further erase the lines of demarcation between the Executive branch and the Judiciary and may very well provoke a constitutional crisis. The relationship between the justice department and a Supreme Court under Chief Justice Roberts would then become pricklier. Is this what Americans want?

But it is not just the department of justice that will be compromised to do the president's bidding. Every Cabinet office will bear the imprint of the president's transactional disposition, especially the Environmental Protection Agency (EPA) and the secretariat of the Interior. He will continue to pour scorn on intelligence reports from the national intelligence agencies. The FBI and the CIA are likely to come under greater scrutiny with a view to getting them to conform to the new normal under Trump. The Department of Homeland Security will be emboldened to step up its activities in detaining and deporting undocumented persons, only this time around the activities of agencies like the Immigration and Customs Enforcement (ICE) will become more aggressive, repulsive and mercurial. I could go on, but you get the picture.

4. **Further widening of the economic inequality gap.** President Trump has promised that he will move for another tax cut in his second term. One does not doubt that if he is re-elected this will be the first order of business on his economic reform agenda. You do not have to ask who would be the greater beneficiaries of this tax cut- the richest people in the country. We have seen this movie before. The only thing that would

stand between him and a next tax heist for the rich is a divided Congress or one controlled by the Democrats.

Even if there is not a tax heist, Trump will not pay any attention to the growing income inequality in the country. Despite his pretensions to the contrary, he has no stomach for this fight. He would not hesitate to gut any safety net for the poor if it means diverting money, by executive orders, to his pet projects. Social Security and other entitlement programs would come under greater assault.

So, the prospects of a better life for struggling middle class families will become harder and more desperate. They will be working harder than they have ever worked without any real possibility of a hopeful future. There will be greater economic despair as the full brunt of the Covid-19 economic fallout bears down on their shoulders.


## 5. Greater peril with the escalation of climate change.

If there is one reason why all young voters should reject President Trump on November 3, this is it. There are two existential threats that we face in our time-a global pandemic of the kind we are now experiencing and climate change, both of which are not unrelated. Because if Mr. Trump wins a second term, he and his Republican science deniers will not suddenly get an epiphany that they should now become stout defenders of the environment.

We can expect further rollbacks of regulations that have prevented the despoilation of the environment. The administration will become more aggressive in promoting and implementing policies aimed at increasing fossil fuel explorations in such places as the Arctic National Wildlife Refuge (ANWR) in Alaska. He will seek to do this by executive orders which he sees as a speedier way of fulfilling his wishes. He will do everything in his power to ensure that his fossil fuel enablers get the permits they need to do drilling and fracking. The governor of Florida, Ron Desantis, would have two years remaining in office. I would expect Trump to force his hand to allow for offshore drilling for oil, a matter, to his credit, former governor Rick Scott opposed.

More and more acres of real estate that was protected for wildlife and other recreational activities are likely to be plundered under a Trump second term. As he did with the Paris Climate Accord, he will further isolate America from participation in any global effort to protect the environment. There will be protests and lawsuits from concerned groups and even Congress, but Trump will be at his bullying best as he uses the bully pulpit to trumpet and further his cause. His re-election will represent the greatest assault on the integrity of the environment in our lifetime.

By the way, with the planet heating more every year and with the possibilities of more destructive fires as we have seen in the West Coast of the United States, the Amazon forest and other areas, deforestation is taking place at an alarming level. It would be prudent for the United Nations to give this closer attention. I would suggest that this body declares an International Tree Planting Day, just as we have for other worthy global causes. This would focus the world on an aggressive reforestation project each year which can only inure to a healthier planet for all of us.

6. **Greater alliance with dictators, and other right-wing populist leaders around the world**. President Trump may in fact see himself as the de facto leader of this right-wing populist movement. More of these governments are likely to emerge. The leaders of those that already exist will tighten their grip on power as an America under Trump could be relied upon to turn a blind eye to their abuse of their citizens. He would be the fodder for their worst dictatorial sensibilities and would want to assert those for himself in America as well.

At the risk of repetition here, his relationship with Putin has been well documented. In a second-term this relationship will be on steroids. Putin will be more emboldened to take on his neighbors; his aggression toward the Ukraine is likely to be more troublesome. Frankly, I am worried about how safe the nation's most important military and intelligence secrets will be under a Trump second term. I suspect that many others, especially in the military and intelligence communities, are equally worried. Muted silence would not be an option if one's fears should be realized.

7. **Further deterioration of America's standing in the world.** This is almost a given. By the end of Trump's first term, whatever is left of America's alliances in the world, will be put under more severe strain. Many of these may break or evaporate permanently. As I said in a previous chapter, Trump

has been successful in already tearing up some of these treaties and international obligations that America, in good faith and good sense, signed on to. We do so as the most powerful country in the world and because the world instinctively expects us to. Thus, our lead in the Paris climate accord was a no-brainer.

In a Trump second term his reckless disregard for these international obligations will put them at further risk. Winning will convince him that he was on the right path in the first term. He can then continue on this path, but in a more aggressive mode. He would be the world emperor and would throw his weight around. Expect more world tensions as a result.

The work of the Trump administration in brokering peace between the United Arab Emirates and Bahrain and Israel is significant. Seeking peace at any time in the notoriously volatile Middle East is a good thing. So, while this is a step in the right direction, one cannot help but see a germ of suspicion in the move. So, I ask some questions. Is it mere coincidence that it should come at this particular time when we are on the cusp of the November elections? Is it a move to shore up the president's image and to present him as a leader on the world stage? Also, is it coincidental that peace between two Arab countries and Israel is being brokered by a president who has not hidden his desire to win the Nobel Peace Prize, whose winner is usually announced in the month of October? I am just asking these questions aloud as given the president's transactional nature, he is going to be thinking about what is in it for him, and how best he can benefit from this engagement. The reader can fill out the blanks.

It is interesting that while the global community has largely welcomed this peace effort, there has not been any uproarious applause for the effort. Why? Is it that people are waiting to see what will truly come of this accord and are suspending judgment to ascertain whether they were entered into in good faith or predicated to give the president a boost in the elections? Again, just asking.


**8. Continued belligerence, falsehoods and exhaustion of the nation.** Anyone who believes that Mr. Trump will change his modus operandi and behave more gently or humanely in a second term is living in the land of Oz. The president's belligerence toward those who criticize him will continue apace. So will his falsehoods and abominable tweets, his ascribing names and epithets to perceived enemies, and his further shattering of the norms of decency that have held this country together.

The country has become exhausted by the constant carping, whining and complaining that comes from the president. It is exhausted by the constant inattention to details and the consequent drift of the country towards anarchy. It is exhausted by a chief executive who seems to delight in chaos as a governing principle, and who believes that his way of doing things is always the right way, as he alone can fix things.

The country must ask whether this, among other worse excesses by the government, is something they can live with for the next four years. In former years, any of the issues mentioned above would be sufficient to render a president wounded in office. But for about 40 percent of Americans, they are prepared to live with it. This is particularly true of single or double issue voters. Those who are committed to the view that Joe Biden will cause socialism to dominate America, may not vote for him. Those who believe that abortion is immoral will vote for Mr. Trump. Many of these are in the evangelical camp, yet they will suspend their moral judgments on the president's obvious immoral behavior in office as long as their pet issue will be protected. They will be more outraged at the president not getting a chance to make a nomination for the Supreme Court than they would be about children being separated from their parents on the Southern border.

I would urge an openness to a wider set of issues. The burden of this book has been to highlight some of these issues so that voters can have a more informed view of what can happen if Mr. Trump is elected to a second term. What is clear is that this election cannot be based on one or two issues but a panoply of issues for so many things are at stake. The very future of the country is at stake. Will the country in voting for a more secure future for their children and grandchildren, make the right choice? If what they have experienced in this first term of Trump is not what they believe America is about, will they have the moral conviction to say to him on November 3, "Mr. president, you're fired!"

# CHAPTER SEVEN

## A MAN WEIGHED IN THE BALANCE AND FOUND WANTING

*"MENE, MENE, TEKEL, PARSIN" God has numbered the days of your kingdom and brought it to an end; you have been weighed on the scales and found wanting*-Daniel 5: 26, 27.

According to Old Testament history, around 538 B.C. Belshazzar, king of Babylon and successor to the notorious and feared Nebuchadnezzar, held a party in his court for his princes, his wives and his concubines. He ordered that the golden and silver vessels which his father had taken out of the temple in Jerusalem be brought in so that his guests would drink wine from them. This was not just a mockery of God and Jewish culture, but it was a barefaced attempt by an autocratic king to demonstrate his unfettered power to his friends and the people at large.

His hubris and perhaps narcissism were clear for all to see. As he and his guests carried on with their drunken orgy, a finger suddenly appeared and wrote on the wall, "mene, mene, tekel, parsin" (or upharsisn as some translators have it). Daniel, one of the young and promising men that had been taken into exile in Babylon, and who had proven his loyalty to Yahweh, was called in to interpret the writing on the wall. The interpretation was no comfort to the king. His kingdom would be taken from him. He, the king, had been weighed in the balance and found wanting. Daniel would not hide the truth from the autocratic center of power in his time.

And neither should we in ours. As I reflected on this story, I could not help but see haunting parallels to where we are in America today where Trump is concerned. There may be no finger writing on a wall, but the words addressed to Belshazzar and his courtiers, ring with unerring accuracy in describing America under the Trump administration.

If the polls are to be believed, they consistently tell the story of a once proud nation in decline, of a country that seems impotent to restrain the propensities of a man who no doubt harbors the dispositions of the autocratic Belshazzar. While he may not be drinking sacrilegiously from holy vessels taken from a temple, (the president says he does not drink alcohol), he has caused the nation to be drinking from a chalice of the bitter gall of unnecessary suffering and pain brought on by his mishandling of the nation's affairs, especially in the area of the raging pandemic.

The finger is writing on the wall and what it is writing is no different than that which filled ancient Belshazzar with fear and dread. November 3, 2020 is the day of reckoning. It is not just a day of reckoning for the Trump presidency, but for the American people and whether it can survive as a democratic project for the next four years if he should be re-elected.

By any metric we choose, Mr. Trump has been weighed in the balance and found terribly wanting. Like all would-be autocrats before him, he has no one else to blame but himself. I have said repeatedly that he is his worst enemy; that by his words and actions he has judged and declared himself for who he is: an inept, incompetent, erratic and irascible president more concerned about his own fortunes than those of the country he claims to love.

As a result, close to sixty percent or more of the people whom he has governed for almost four years have declared him an inept and incompetent president. They have weighed him in the scales of probity and are now convinced that the Kingdom of America that he would like to build in his own image must be laid to rest. His kingdom, set on a foundation of racial bigotry and a confederate past that many Americans would wish to leave behind, is not the America they want to live in.

What are we to make of the finger writing on the wall today? What message are we reading? As I think about these questions, I get the numbing feeling that too many Americans are detached from the reality of life around them. There are those, rightly so, who will be concerned about their pet issues or project, such as abortion or the nomination of the next Supreme Court justice. But they would ignore other large issues as Mr. Trump's too cozy relationship with Mr. Putin, or the termination of the Affordable Care Act which would imperil the health of millions with pre-existing conditions.

They will be vehemently concerned about Mr. Biden's tilt towards socialism or him being a pawn of Senator Bernie Sanders, as one elderly voter told me, while at the same time being lukewarm to Mr. Trump's obvious disregard for the rule of law. Because we are such a divided country, issues become more sharply contested as people are labeled and consigned to competing camps.

But we are in a gigantic battle for the soul of this country. This is a time for all Americans of good will to seriously ponder whether, with all fidelity to their pet issues, America as we have seen it over the past three years and counting, is that which represents the best of what is in the American spirit and soul. Whether for the next four years the country will not be irrevocably changed for the worse if the present status quo should persist. This is an existential question that will be answered by every voter who votes on November 3, 2020.

As this consideration weighs on my mind, I am reminded of the oft quoted statement attributed to the 17th century political philosopher Edmund Burke, that the only thing necessary for evil to triumph is for good people to do nothing. But who are the good people in America today? Who are those who are sitting by while right before their very eyes mendacity is becoming a regulatory and governing principle in a country founded on democratic principles; the free press is declared fake by a president who brooks no criticism of himself; the nations troops, in a report from the nation's intelligence agencies, are being threatened in a theater of war by bounties being placed on their heads by an adversary power; the president openly rejects the report of his own intelligence agencies and accepts the word of the president of that adversary power, Russia, a man who once headed his country's national intelligence agency, the KGB?

Who is sitting idly detached from reality while in the midst of a raging, easily transmissible respiratory pandemic, the leader of the country can show such reckless disregard for his own life and that of his supporters, by holding indoor campaign rallies where thousands of people are assembled, and many, including himself, not wearing masks? And this when it is a universally accepted fact that wearing masks is one of the most effective ways of preventing the spread of the virus and keeping people alive?

Who is sitting on the fence while in the midst of this pandemic the president and his Republican enablers are supporting a brief in the Supreme Court that may very well terminate the healthcare act and thus remove health insurance from millions of people and millions more who have and will lose their jobs in the near future? And this, even if those millions could get insurance, may find it too expensive to purchase or be denied coverage because of a pre-existing condition.

Who is sitting idly consumed by his or her own problems not to notice the president's debasement of the institutions of the country-from his castigating of service men and women in the military, to his clear attempts at politicizing the department of justice, and his placing his people in departments of government who are clearly there to carry out his wishes even if these are injurious to the public good? And this, while the president indulges a litany of boisterous tweets which often showcase his obsession with self and his contempt for perceived enemies.

I could go on, but the picture is clear. I know how difficult it is when things are so hard for so many Americans for them to be focused on the implications of Trumpian behavior for the future of their country. But I would urge them nonetheless to pay a little more attention this time around for we are in perilous times. We must not believe that America cannot go the way of other empires before it. In fact, there are those who see the haunting specter of what led to the demise of the Roman Empire in America today. The Roman Empire fell largely from the rot that had set in within. By the time the Barbarian invasions occurred the seeds of its destruction had already been sown. It was a weakened shell, morally and economically. Whatever might have defined its might and power as an empire had died as the empire descended into moral bankruptcy and became a mere shell of its former self.

And what about Germany? Germany was hardly an empire like Rome. By the time Hitler rose to power, it had been humiliated in the Treaty of Versailles after the First World War. After the war, Germany was an economic basket case, but it was still a country defined by its rich history, traditions in science, medicine, arts and culture.

Hitler's rise to power in Germany did not happen by chance or overnight. It was a gradual and progressive chipping away at the institutions of government that survived the First World War. It was a systematic undermining of the press and other organs of democracy by propaganda and blatant falsehoods that too many bought into. Too many people were supinely silent, even in the church, while Hitler consolidated power especially after the burning of the Reichstag building in 1933. Many were silent when he annexed the Sudetenland, invaded Poland and set the stage for his domination of Europe. Many twiddled their thumbs and were distracted by their own preoccupations when Hitler started his assault on the Jewish population, first in Germany and then in Europe, ending in his final solution and the decimation of millions of Jews.

Those who carried out the atrocities against the Jews in Hitler's concentration camps were people who got up in the morning, brushed their teeth, combed their hair and went to work. They no doubt had coffee or wine while the acrid smell of burning bodies in the crematoria wafted through the air.

I paint this picture because we should never be deluded that America cannot go the way of the Roman Empire and Germany if we are not vigilant. Some Americans do not seem to like when comparisons are made between actions by their leaders such as president Trump and what happened in Germany, even though these actions bear almost copycat resemblance to what is happening in America. We would have to be naïve to think that what happened in Germany cannot happen here. That the worst egregious acts of a narcissistic leader which compromised the integrity of German democracy, co-opted an unwary and non-vigilant citizenry in its atrocities, cannot be America's experience, especially when we see these same tendencies in our own president.

There is good reason why the Germans insist on teaching the subject of the Holocaust and the Nazi era in their schools and allow students to visit concentration camp sites,

Holocaust memorials or museums. They do so to help the present and future generations to be cognizant of the atrocities of an earlier generation that embarrassed the nation by its inhumanity to its fellowmen. They do not hide their shame but face it, with the understanding that these things are capable of reasserting themselves in the future and that this should never again happen.

## A Message to the Democrats

Any successful weighing of President Trump in the scales of justice, moral probity and competence in running the affairs of the country, must consider the message of those who would want to replace him. The Biden-Harris ticket has an uphill task. They are battling against a president who does not believe that any rule applies to him and who seems not to recognize any bound of moral decency in achieving his objectives. His enmity with truth telling is well known. So, between now and November 3, his behavior is likely to get more erratic and aggressive and they have to be prepared.

They do not have to follow ever smoke signal of distraction that the president sends their way. He is notorious for setting political fires, and while they have to address the most dangerous of these fires, they have to be careful they are not sidetracked by attempting to put them out and so neglect their own messaging to the people. This is part of Trump's playbook to divide and create enough chaos to keep them pinned down. They must not allow themselves to be lured into this trap.

It is all about messaging and the extent to which you are able to get your listeners to buy into it. One of the reasons why Trump's base is so committed to him is that they really believe what he tells them, even though his statements are often pregnant with falsehoods and go against their best interests. So, he has a distinct advantage here. From here he can only hope to pick off enough independents and wavering Democrats to get enough Electoral College votes to ease into the finishing line.

So, there is a kind of monolithic support that Trump enjoys that is not available to former Vice-president Biden and Senator Harris. The Democratic Party has a wide tent with diverse constituencies and contending interests. For example, the progressive group has shown itself to be fiercely independent. Even though their putative leader, Senator Bernie Sanders, has given his support to the Biden-Harris ticket, any fierce loyalty to the Biden program cannot be assumed. The attempt by Trump to label Biden a socialist who will wreck the economy is derived largely from the posturing of the progressive movement in the party.

The one good thing for the Democratic ticket is that all factional groups in the party seem united in the one effort to make Trump a one term president. But even then, nothing must be assumed. While the planets seem aligned in their favor, they must remember who they are dealing with and take nothing for granted. There will be no slam dunk and every vote must be striven for. And this, inevitably, has to do with the kind of messaging that comes from the party.

This message has to be tight, simple and more pointed to meet the existential needs of the audience being addressed. What do I mean by this? People already know that Trump is corrupt, indulges in lies as a principle of governing, and is perhaps the most disgusting president of their lifetimes. This knowledge is already baked into the minds of voters. There is no need to waste precious time between now and November 3 reminding them of this, especially when the candidates are making stump speeches.

They have to focus on a few initiatives that affect people directly and that can affect their future in the near term. Three of these issues are the pandemic and the allied need to save the Affordable Care Act; the growing impoverishment of the middle class, jobs and growing income inequality; and racial justice and harmony in the society. I would consider these in the order they are given.

You notice I did not mention the environment as one of these key issues. While I recognize the importance of this subject, between now and November, people do not consider this as germane to their immediate pain and suffering as much as the three mentioned above. I may be wrong, but many people see climate change as an esoteric subject which does not preoccupy their minds as s much as the pandemic, healthcare, their economic livelihoods, and racial justice do. People living in Oregon, California and other areas where wildfires have destroyed life and property, may be more concerned about the climate change argument because they are directly affected, but between now and election day, to what extent is the larger population concerned? So, I would urge the Democrats that while they should not ignore the environmental problem, in the short time they have, there is more to be gained focusing on what I would call these existential issues.

And the messaging needs to be more pointed and direct. Sometimes candidates assume that everybody knows what they are talking about. Because your message is simple it does not mean that you have necessarily communicated it. It must speak to the heart, to the pain that people are feeling and the future disruptions in their lives that a particular policy may cause. Specific demographics demand a more targeted approach.

Take Florida, for example. There is a large, elderly, retired population which has been seen to be loyal to the Republican Party. The Biden team has been able to make inroads into this population and has reduced the president's lead among these voters. There are two issues that preoccupy this elderly population-healthcare/Medicare and social security. In targeting this population, the Democratic message needs to spell out how much a danger a second Trump administration poses to these subjects. And there are tangible reasons to be concerned. The health of many in the sunshine state has been, and still is being imperiled by Covid-19. Many have died or have been permanently sickened by it. The argument must be constantly hammered home to this population that this did not have to happen and if the president is given a second term, worse will follow.

As important as climate change is to Florida, between now and November, this subject does not occupy as important a place in people's minds as do healthcare and social security. The president's untruths that he cares about social security must be vigorously exposed to this population. Not many people know that the payroll tax funds the social security program. The Biden campaign should explain what are the likely implications for their social security payments if the Trump administration should defund it. And he made clear recently by executive order where he stands on this matter when he suspended payroll tax deductions until the end of the year. Is this the actions of a person who means the elderly well? Biden himself should pay a visit to the Republican bastion in the Villages in Florida and talk about these subjects. It should be an essential part of his Florida initiative leading up to the elections.

While on the subject of healthcare in Florida, the Biden ticket should emphasize more pointedly to people how they will be affected if the Affordable Care Act is terminated. Many people may not know that Trump and his Republican allies now have a brief in the Supreme Court that may end the Act as we know it. By a 5-4 vote it could disappear. What then of pre-existing conditions for the wide population? We would return to a time when millions will be denied coverage on the basis of a pre-existing condition, among which the almost 700,000 people who have contracted Covid-19 in Florida so far, would be numbered. And bear in mind that the Florida legislature under Republican control with two Republican governors (Rick Scott and Ron Desantis), unconscionably and wickedly, never expanded the Medicaid program as was allowed under the ACA. Consider the number of poor people who got sicker or died because they had no health coverage. This behavior on the part of the Republicans is one that continues to live in infamy and Democrats should pound them relentlessly on this. The airwaves should be inundated with advertisements highlighting the grave danger many will face if Trump is given a second term. The Republicans are clearly vulnerable on these subjects.

Pointing out Trump's character flaws which are already a given will not hold as much traction as the immediate pain and suffering that Floridians are experiencing in their healthcare and the ongoing threat to their economic livelihood. It is the absence of the explanation of the existential threat that these things can have on people's lives that is lacking in the message. That is where most people in the population are itching most. That is where Democrats need to scratch more. They must pull the people into a conversation with themselves about these things and convince them that they are the ones who are best able to deliver for them from 2021 onward.

And speaking about conversation, I would suggest to the Democrats that they have equally pointed conversations with people, especially in the rural areas of the swing states-in Michigan, Wisconsin, Pennsylvania and Florida-about these and other matters. I know the limitations imposed by the Covid-19 pandemic on traveling and in-person meetings, so I would recommend what I call fireside chats, not unlike those done by President Franklyn D. Roosevelt in an earlier time. These would be in the form of two to three-minute advertisements featuring talks given by Joe Biden himself. With his homespun, folksy and affable characteristics, there is no one more capable of conducting these chats. These should air regularly in these areas.

## Ruth Bader Ginsburg

As I wound up the final pages of this book news came of the death of Supreme Court Justice, Ruth Bader Ginsburg. I can think of no better way to close this book than that of paying tribute to her for her life and work that literally transformed this nation. It I hard to speak of her in the past tense, but she was the epitome of the noblest and best of what of what America is.

She was a champion for women rights on the bench and in larger life. She helped the ordinary person to understand that the law was not an abstract principle that was detached from his or her daily reality. She believed intensely in social justice and the rights of the downtrodden. She was passionate that women should have sovereignty over their own bodies and that the state should not trespass on these rights. And she did so in such a way as to endear her fellow citizens to her to the point of becoming a pop icon in a culture where justice is often a cloistered virtue.

She fought debilitating cancer bravely and as long as she could to ensure that she could continue her work on the Supreme Court. In the context of divided politics in Washington, she was acutely aware why she had to be there. This has become more obvious since her death. The president and the Leader of the Senate, Mitch McConnell, are anxious to fill her seat. The best tribute that could be paid to her is to honor her dying wish that her replacement is not done until there is a new president in office. This should not be something too difficult to ask for, but will the Republicans who control the Senate have the integrity, moral fortitude and generosity of spirit to adhere to her wishes. Meanwhile, rest well thou good and faithful servant. You have done your work well and future generations will call you blessed.

## POSTCRIPT
## LETTER TO MY GRANDCHILDREN

My Dear Darlings,

I am writing this letter to you to tell you how much I love you. Like mommy and daddy, grandma and I are very proud of the beautiful persons you are becoming. You are so well behaved and obedient to your parents.

I want to also tell you that you live in a beautiful country. In fact, it is one of the most beautiful places on this planet, blessed with rolling hills, mighty rivers, beautiful coastlines and amazing forests. It is also blessed with amazing people who have come here from all over the world. If you work hard, you have the opportunity for greatness and to become a useful and productive citizen.

Although this country has been greatly blessed, it has not always lived up to the things that can make it truly great. As I write to you, my heart is very heavy with sadness at how the country is failing to live up to the best of what it is capable. Mommy and daddy have spoken to you of the Covid-19 pandemic, why you have to be wearing masks and why you have to be staying at home to do your schooling. I know this has been hard on you because you miss your friends, especially playing outside with them.

But this is a very dangerous virus and over 200,000 people have died from it as I write. Close to seven million have been infected and many may not recover their good health for a long time. I tell you this not to frighten your little hearts, because I know you will be alright. But I do so because I am sad as I know that things did not have to be like this. Many children your age have lost grandmas and grandpas, aunts, uncles, brothers, sisters and their little friends. But I will not weary your little minds to explain why. Perhaps when grandma and I are able to see you again we can talk about this some more. One thing I can tell you is that we miss seeing you and giving you a big hug. But we hope we will be able to do that soon.

There are other things that are not going too well in this great country. It is true that you live in the richest country in the world, but so many are poor even though they work hard. What is also true is that when you get older and you get your license to drive, you are likely to be stopped on the road because of the color of your skin. You are likely to be stopped three times more than the white kids in your classes. It is not their fault, but that of a system which for years has victimized people of our color.

Also, I am concerned about what the scientists call climate change, which has to with the heating of the planet and the danger to life in the environment in which you live. This is a big one and I want you to pay keen attention to it as you grow older. Do your part to keep your space clean and encourage others to do so as well.

There are many other things that are wrong with this great land, but your little minds cannot grasp them now. There will be time for this as you grow older. Only pardon me for being so wordy, my little darlings, but you know grandpa, always wanting you to learn something new.

Daddy, mommy, grandma and I have always taught you to show respect for other people and to treat others fairly as you want to be treated yourselves; to never look down on other people unless you are picking them up; to work hard for what you need and not to cut corners; to show respect to people, especially your elders, and never to cause those around you to feel small because of something that you may say or do to them.

We believe that these are the values that will help you best to grow strong and purposeful in the society. They and others like them will give your life a sense of meaning. You can only get so much out of life as you are willing to put into it. Never take anything for granted, and be always willing to help someone along the way.

I have no doubt that you will grow up to be good and productive citizens of this great country. I see you as future leaders, standing proudly to help others to a better future. The country will need you and your friends to do your part to make it better, more loving and gentler. It is a future that beckons your generation to guide it to a better place.

Mommy, daddy, grandma and I know that you will not fail us. Your young, fertile minds will see to that. Your good behavior and hard work will ensure that you become the best you are capable of. I will pray for God's protection and guidance over your precious lives. Only know this, we love you with all our hearts.
With lots of love,
Grandpa.

# ABOUT THE AUTHOR

The Rev. Dr. Raulston Nembhard is a retired priest of the Episcopal/Anglican Church. He has earned degrees from the University of the West Indies, Yale Divinity School, Stetson University and the Reformed Theological Seminary. He is a trained Marriage, Couples and Family Therapist
He is the author of:

**Muslim Rage and Christian Arrogance: A Time for Reason Repentance and Dialogue**

**Finding Peace in the Midst of Life's Storms**

**Your Self-esteem guide to a Better Life**

**Radical Obedience and Discipleship in the Theology of Dietrich Bonhoeffer**

**Beyond Petulance: Republican Politics and the Future of America**

...................................................................

For consultation and speaking engagements please contact Dr. Nembhard:stead6655@aol.com.Website:www.drraulston.com